W9-BCE-819

160° 150° 140° 130° 40° 30° 20° 10° 0° 10° 20° 30° 40°

The Oregon Country

CALIFORNIA

MEXICAN POSSESSIONS

C OCEAN

WAIIAN IS. (Sandwich IS.)

Oahu
Hawaii

The South Seas

0   200   500   800   1000
60° 40°   20° 50°
0°
EQUATOR
Statute Miles

enix Islands
nton I.
Phoenix I.

Marquesas Islands

ion
oup

a IS.

IS.

Palmerston Atoll
COOK ISLANDS

SOCIETY ISLANDS

Tahiti

TUAMOTU ISLANDS

Austral IS.

Pitcairn I.

Easter I.

PACIFIC OCEAN

160° 150° 140° 130° 120° 110°

NEW ENGLAND
AND THE SOUTH SEAS

HARVARD UNIVERSITY PRESS

NEW ENGLAND
AND THE SOUTH SEAS

ERNEST S. DODGE

AMBRIDGE, MASSACHUSETTS 1965

Distributed in Great Britain by Oxford University Press, London

Library of Congress Catalog Card Number 65-19823

Printed in the United States of America

TO
TWO NEW ENGLANDERS
WHO HAVE BEEN THERE
MY CHILDREN
REBECCA AND STANLEY
AND TO THE MEMORY OF
BEATRICE

PREFACE

This book is in substance a series of eight lectures given before the Lowell Institute in Boston during February 1962. The genesis of these lectures lay in a web of planned and fortuitous circumstances that were a part of my experience for over a quarter of a century. As a coastal New Englander, satisfied with his geographical lot, I was lucky at an early age to drift into a line of work that suited my nature and satisfied my interests. The Peabody Museum of Salem contains within its walls a combination of material—natural and ethnological, maritime and archival—that is unique in this country, if not in the world. As the junior member of a staff of four in this impecunious but basically lusty institution in the early thirties, I was given one odd chore after another in all of the departments—a variety of work that appealed to my conservative but restless temperament.

It is not easy for one raised by the seaside, where most of his ancestors have for generations gotten their livelihood, to wash the sound of the rote from his ears or the smell of the mudflats from his nostrils. I had no desire to, and a maritime museum beside the sea was exactly my kettle of fish. But this was not the only favorable aspect of the place. Even as a boy I had an absorbing interest in exotic peoples and cultures. The Peabody had one of the finest ethnological collections in the country, rich in quality and documentation, romantic in origin. The almost instinctive love of his natural surroundings found in most country men, the lore of plant and beast of shore and swale of field and forest was satisfied in the natural history collections of the museum.

When I began specializing on Pacific ethnology another, more romantic, Paradise opened up before me. The South Sea collections of the museum are notable, and those from Polynesia are distinguished. Eventually I published extensively upon them. Soon this ethnological research became augmented by the historical studies. The two went together and there are in the museum library some 850 logbooks and journals with at least an equal number across the street in the Essex Institute. The thriving port of Salem in the late eighteenth and early nineteenth centuries numbered among its most important enterprises that by-product of Far Eastern commerce—the South Seas trade. Relics of that trade—the arts and crafts of the natives; the writings of owners, captains, and sailors; por-traits of the ships and men who participated in it—are rich in the Peabody's collections. From the local resources the trail led beyond to the other towns and institutions of our seaboard, to Boston, Nantucket, New Bedford, and the Connecticut shore; to its beginnings in England; and to Tahiti, the Fijis, and Hawaii—the South Seas themselves. I became fascinated by the long, in some respects close, relation between the two regions.

These lectures were planned to emphasize certain common facets of New England and South Sea history, and the eco-nomic, cultural, religious, and political effect of the one region upon the other—but especially of Yankee influence in the Pacific. There is a mass of material relating to this subject and, in order to remain within the required time limits, it was neces-sary to touch some subjects in a summary manner and telescope others more than might be ideally desirable. The material used is based upon selected works from the vast literature on the Pacific listed in the bibliography, on unpublished manuscripts mostly in the Peabody Museum of Salem, and upon personal observation made during an extensive trip to the Society Islands, Fijis, and Hawaii in 1957.

The subject is enormous and the time it would take to produce a definitive history on this topic is not available to me at present. The literature on the subject is vast and the unpublished sources even larger. It seemed desirable to print these lectures much as they were given. Incidents and personalities have often been selected as typical of certain events and men. For each trader or whaler there were hundreds of others, and for each missionary or politician, dozens more who had similar experiences.

I wish to thank the authorities of the Lowell Institute and to acknowledge the encouragement of the trustees and staff of the Peabody Museum of Salem. The staffs of The Massachusetts Historical Society, the Boston Athenaeum, and Harvard College Library have been infinitely kind. Houghton Mifflin Company courteously granted permission to quote from W. C. Ford, ed., *Letters of Henry Adams (1858-1891)*. Many good friends have contributed to my research, and I am especially grateful to Eugenia Ford for her patience in deciphering my tortuous manuscripts.

Ernest S. Dodge

Marblehead, Massachusetts
May 5, 1964

CONTENTS

ILLUSTRATIONS

(Unless otherwise stated all photographs are courtesy of the Peabody Museum of Salem.)

NEW ENGLAND AND THE SOUTH SEAS

ILLUSTRATIONS

NEW ENGLAND
AND THE SOUTH SEAS

I ~

THE GREAT SOUTH SEA

New England and the South Seas are half a world away from each other—the one a cramped continental corner, the other magnificently oceanic. Geographically they are far apart. But they share one great geographical feature. The sea, only feasible means of reaching distant places in a reasonable length of time available to mankind before the airplane shrunk the world, links them.

Climatically the regions are just as diverse. New England with its temperamental climate, now drenching in rain, now freezing to the marrow, and now broiling the unwary sunbather lobster-red, is no kin of high volcanic islands or palm-fringed coral rings under bright and clement sunshine. Grey, white-topped North Atlantic rollers do not resemble the long, blue, undulating swells of the Pacific.

Nor can one see much kinship between the New Englander, a breed physically and mentally toughened by his country, his beliefs, his inheritance, and his institutions; and the Polynesian, gaily obliging, irresponsible, agreeable, and, at the same time, cruel, sometimes cannibalistic, and vengeful. For all their disparity these creatures of opposite environments share certain characteristics. If the New Englander was dry and taciturn, his religious representative, the missionary, in his professional and zealous verbosity could be as long-winded as any Samoan "talking chief"; and Yankee and South Sea Islander alike were, each in his particular craft, masters of seamanship and sailors extraordinary. New Englanders could and did take their ships anywhere in the world, and South Sea Islanders sailed their long, twin-hulled canoes across thousands of miles of Pacific emptiness.

It is difficult to see simultaneously in the mind's eye the weathered granite hills and precipitous, volcanic mountains; or the industrious New England harbors of the early nineteenth century and the pass through an atoll or a barrier reef. But different though they were and distant though they be, and while the two peoples are utterly unlike, circumstances of time, history, and economics combined to link them in such a way for nearly a century that the effects of it still linger.

We say tritely that the Pacific is vast, and so it is. The biggest of the world's oceans, it covers more than a third of the earth's surface, an estimated area of about 63,800,000 square miles. It stretches from Bering Strait to the Antarctic ice; along the equator, from Panama to Singapore, it reaches about 11,000 miles, almost half the circumference of the globe.

Not only is this an ocean of immense surface distances, it is equally staggering in its vertical dimensions. Tremendous trenches or deeps slice its bottom and four of these—off the

Philippines, Japan, the Marianas, and Tonga—reach over six miles toward the earth's core. (A deep is any place where the water reaches a depth of more than 18,000 feet or nearly three and one half miles.) The Pacific has more such spots than all other oceans combined. Beneath its waters lie some of the world's greatest mountain ranges, and where the peaks break the surface are treacherous shoals or islands of surpassing loveliness. Of all the ancient features of the earth, the Pacific basin is one of the oldest. Figures of geological time are nearly as enormous as those of astronomical distances and mean as little to most of us. Probably the Pacific hasn't changed much, geologically speaking, for half a billion years, and that is a very long while ago.

The enormous chain of Indonesian Islands—the Philippines, Sumatra, Java, Borneo, Celebes, the Moluccas or Spice Islands, and countless others—form the western perimeter of the Pacific and separate it from the Indian Ocean. Beyond Indonesia, reaching eastward south of the equator, the large islands of the Melanesian chain—New Guinea, the Bismarck Archipelago, the Solomons, New Caledonia, New Hebrides, and the Fijis—reach to the western limits of Polynesia. North of Melanesia and mostly north of the equator, the tiny islands of the Mariana, Caroline, Marshall, and Gilbert groups form the Micronesian chain. All the other populated islands from the Ellice group to Easter and from Hawaii to New Zealand form the Polynesian triangle.

Three types of islands—continental, volcanic, and coral—dominate the Pacific. The great western islands of Indonesia and Melanesia are continental; Sumatra, Java, Borneo, the Philippines, and their neighbors were once part of Asia. As the land submerged or the water rose they were separated from the mainland and from one another. New Guinea, second largest of the world's islands, is a similarly separated chunk of Australia. The seas around continental islands, except near the edge of the continental shelf, are shallow; as islands they are infants—perhaps a scant 40,000 years old. Their flora and fauna are related to that of the parent continents. There is a wealth of species, a richness and variety not found on the oceanic islands.

These oceanic islands are the ones that here concern us. New England commerce with parts of Indonesia was extensive and lucrative but it is another story. The true great basin of the Pacific lies between the continental islands and the Americas where mountains and ridges rise steeply from the vast depths of the ocean bottom. Some of them emerge as spectacular volcanic or high islands of the South Seas and some form the bases for beguiling coral atolls or low islands.

Most of the well known island groups of the Eastern Pacific are of the high mountainous type—old volcanoes that thrust their heads above the ocean surface. Such are the Hawaiian Islands, our fiftieth state, and the Marquesas

1. Tahitian dwelling

where the youthful Melville scrambled over mountain trails. So are the Societies dominated by salubrious, romantic Tahiti; and the Cooks and Australs; Samoa where Stevenson sleeps; Tonga of the brave warriors; the Fijis of the fierce cannibals; and tiny Easter whose monumental remains have provoked more controversy than any other piece of real estate of comparable size.

Volcanic islands are relatively large and time has worn down the masses of basalt. In Hawaii the volcanoes are still active; in others, the Marquesas and Societies for example, they are long dead and have eroded to form some of the most picturesque landscapes in the world. These islands have rivers and streams and alluvial, fertile land. The soil formed by the weathering is rich; food plants such as breadfruit, coconut, plaintain, taro, sweet potatoes, and numerous fruits grow easily and in abundance. Thus, along the coasts and up the river valleys, high islands are able to support a dense population. High islands may have fringing reefs which lie close inshore to the coastal plain, barrier reefs at varying distances offshore with sheltered lagoons rich in fish, or no reefs at all. Some like Tahiti have good passes through barrier reefs into safe sheltered lagoons; others like the Cooks have only fringing reefs or shallow passes which prohibit the entry of ships. Outside the reefs the bottom drops to precipitous depths which no anchor cable will reach and visiting vessels must lie off and on, a dangerous proceeding at best. The Marquesas have no reefs at all, but there are suitable harbors. High islands have more varieties of food-producing plants are able to support heavier populations than their coral neighbors.

Coral islands typify the popular concept of South Sea isles of romance. They have grown on the tops of isolated volcanic mountains that do not reach the surface or in shallows formed by ridges of high land beneath the ocean. Corals are polyps (known collectively as Madreporaria) which precipitate a lime skeleton. This occurs only in tropical waters, for the coral polyps cannot flourish in water colder than 68° Fahrenheit, nor can they live constructively at much more than twenty fathoms. Within the limitations of warm, shallow water the coral-producing anemone flourish and the reefs build u p.

A reef on a submerged volcanic mountain top enclosi ng a central lagoon forms the classical coral atoll. Such a reef is usually irregular, with islets strung along it like beads. Normally one or more openings break its rim, enabling vessels to sail into the sheltered anchorage of its lagoon. Seldom do es an atoll have the symmetry seen illustrated in old geography and dictionary diagrams. The Central Polynesian name for a reef islet is "motu" and most coral islands consist of a series of motu connected by flat-topped reefs awash at high tide and exposed at low water. On islands of this kind food plants, except for coconuts, are neither as abundant, as various, nor as productive as on high volcanic islands.

A variant of the coral atoll is the raised coral island. Niue is the largest example, but the phosphate-producing islands of Nauru, Ocean, and Makatea are the most spectacular. Once coral atolls, they were heaved high in the air by a great cata-clysm. Niue is about two hundred feet high, while the cliffs of Makatea rise in rough pock-marked walls for three hundre d feet.* Each of these islands is depressed in the middle, the old lagoon bottom. At the foot of the cliffs there is a narrow shel lf where the native population lives in palm-thatched villages. From the shelf's edge the shore drops precipitously to grea t depths.

The climates of the Pacific's surrounding coasts and the

* In 1957 I was at Makatea while the freighter *Pioneer Reef* unloaded oil for the phosphate company. The island is an interesting and spectacular natural phenomenon. Since docks cannot be built because of the water's depth, a ship must moor to a complicated series of buoys, and be pulled in from one series to another until within about a hundred yards of the shore. A small square harbor for small boats has been blasted out of the coral rock. High above, the cantil ever, an enormous contraption, extends its telescoping length over the ship and takes a hose as hore. Nearby the funicular railway, rising at a forty-five-degree angle, takes one to the top of the cliffs to a roadway where one can walk or take a narrow-gauge railroad to the phosphate work s and village of native laborers.

NEW ENGLAND AND THE SOUTH SEAS

islands within its basin are not only affected by latitude, ranging as it does from polar to equatorial conditions, but also by the main ocean currents which sweep around in great circular patterns, clockwise in the Northern Hemisphere and counterclockwise in the Southern. These currents, together with the prevailing winds, may cause coldness, warmth, moisture, or dryness far different from what might be expected from latitude alone. Equally important to the consequence of currents on climate is their effect on the distribution of sea life.

Mankind relies upon two kinds of regular Pacific winds. The monsoons, blowing from the cool water across the warm land, bring the rainy season to southeastern Asia, make the land more bountiful, and benefit millions of people. In the winter the winds reverse direction, producing an opposite drying effect. Even more important are the trade winds. The dependability of trade winds provided the motive power of commerce as long as the sailing ship was the essential carrier. There are four belts of these winds. The westerly trades of the North Pacific, between 30° and 60°, were the principal sailing route from Asia to North America. Spain's Manila galleons, returning from the Philippines to Acapulco, Mexico, in the late sixteenth century, followed this passage. South of these but still north of the equator lie the northeast trades, and, south of the equator, the southeast trades. These were the easterlies picked up by ships crossing the ocean westward. Below the southeast trades lies another belt of strong westerlies called by sailors from their strength and latitude, "The Roaring Forties."

❊

Conveniently, the islands of the Pacific are grouped into three great areas, based on the kinds of people that inhabit them rather than upon natural geographical divisions.

THE GREAT SOUTH SEA

Melanesia (the black islands) is inhabited by the Oceanic negroids; Polynesia (the many islands), by a pleasant, brown, partially Caucasoid race; and Micronesia (the tiny islands), by a racially mixed people akin to the Polynesians but with more oriental affinities.

Melanesians, with related Papuans, live on the large islands and groups which stretch eastward from Indonesia south of the equator, including New Guinea, the Bismarck Archipelago, the Solomons, New Hebrides, New Caledonia, and Fiji. In general, Papuan-speaking peoples live in the interior of New Guinea and some of the other larger islands while the coasts are inhabited by Melanesian speakers. However, the languages and dialects are many and frequently the inhabitants of adjacent villages cannot talk to each other. The peoples of Melanesia are the least known of any in Oceania or, for that matter, in the world. It is a difficult region to work in and few serious anthropological studies were made there until the twentieth century. Even today villages that have never been seen by white men are being discovered in the interior of New Guinea. Aside from the fact that the people are all black, use polished stone adzes, bows, and arrows, and domesticate dogs, pigs, and chickens, there is little uniformity in Melanesian culture. The area is ethnologically complicated. Most of the inhabitants indulge in some agriculture, and the coastal dwellers are notable fishers and canoemen. In Fiji, especially in the Lau Islands, there is a mixture of Polynesian blood from Tonga and Samoa, and Fijian material culture is nearly as much Polynesian as Melanesian.

North of the crescent of Melanesian Islands, and mostly north of the equator, lies Micronesia. The islands are small but the groups, which stretch over vast distances, include the Marianas, Carolines, Marshalls, and Gilberts. Typically, they are coral atolls, but the Marianas (formerly called the Ladrones) and some of the Carolines—Yap, Truk, Ponape, and Kusaie—are of either raised limestone or volcanic formation. The Micronesians are a light brown people who speak closely related languages. Their varying island cultures are more uniform than the Melanesians but less so than their Polynesian neighbors to the east. Like other oceanic people they are farmers and fishermen. Marvels of construction, their seagoing canoes were used for voyages to exchange the specialties of different islands.

Polynesia, which extends from Hawaii in the north to New Zealand in the south, and from Tonga in the west to lonely Easter in the east, was the most extensive and at the same time culturally the most homogeneous oceanic area of the three. The language varies only dialectically from group to group and the cultures, though similar, are intriguingly distinctive. Other important island groups within the great triangle are Samoa, Cook, Society, Austral, Tuamotu, and the Marquesas, along with many lesser ones. Polynesians are light brown, physically attractive people, related to Micronesians. They are the South Sea islanders of legend and romance. Theirs are the Pacific paradises of novelist and script writer. Polynesians were farmers and they were also the greatest sailors of them all. Culturally they are classed as neolithic, but only in a material sense, for their religion, social organization, navigation, craftsmanship, and many other aspects of their life was highly developed. They have been studied more extensively than any of the other oceanic peoples, and their origins and migrations have been the subject of endless controversy and dispute.

It is the islands of Polynesia, the Fijis, New Zealand, and Micronesia which most concern us. These are the places frequented by New England whalers, traders, or missionaries.

THE GREAT SOUTH SEA

These are also the healthiest islands for the white man, for here no malaria or other disease strikes him down as in the steaming tropical islands of Melanesia. Consequently, it was at these places that New England missionaries preached, New Bedford whalers refreshed their crews, or Salem traders dickered for sandalwood.

During his Chinese travels in the late thirteenth century, Marco Polo saw the Pacific Ocean from its Asiatic shores. He may have been the first European to do so, but credit for its discovery by a European is given to Balboa, the Spaniard who, crossing the Isthmus of Panama in 1513, saw the blue waters stretching to the horizon. Four days later he reached its shores and claimed it and all the lands washed by it for the Spanish monarchs. Because of the twist in the Isthmus, the new ocean, to Balboa, lay south of the land and he named it the South Sea. Only seven years later Ferdinand Magellan made his famous voyage and in his crossing of the new ocean sailed for thousands of miles with light winds through easy seas, and called it the Pacific. For many years Balboa's name was the more popular and the entire Pacific was known as the Great South Sea; it was not until the second quarter of the nineteenth century that Magellan's name began to replace the more romantic one. But "South Sea" has many connotations. Not only did it once refer to the whole ocean, it also became attached to the Oceanic Islands of the Pacific and to their inhabitants in general. So was it commonly used in the early nineteenth century in New England, and it is so used here.

The exploration of the Pacific following Magellan's crossing of 1520 was very slow. A second Spanish expedition under Loyasa crossed the ocean in Magellan's track in 1526, and a year later another Spaniard named Saavedra sailed from the west coast of Mexico north of the equator with three ships. Two of the ships were lost but Saavedra's flagship, the *Florida,* reached the Philippines. In 1542 and again in 1555 Juan Gaetano sailed from Navidad, Mexico, to the Philippines and returned. Following the first Spanish settlement in the Philippines in 1565, regular voyages between there and Mexico were established for the Manila galleons. Acapulco was the principal port of departure from North America, and the regular route to the Philippines followed the parallel between 12° and 13° north of the equator to Guam, from where the voyage was easily completed. On the return voyage the ships usually sailed at 35° north latitude where the northwesterly winds carried them to the American coast. Because the galleons clung to these favorable established routes across open stretches of ocean, few islands were discovered in the South Pacific during the sixteenth and seventeenth centuries.

Since the first Pacific crossings were all Spanish, so the first planned expeditions into the South Seas were also by navigators of that dominant maritime power. In 1567 the viceroy of Peru, Lopez Garcia de Castro, gave command of an expedition, planned by Pedro Sarmiento de Gamboa, to his nephew Alvaro de Mendaña de Neyra. On November 19 of that year, Mendaña sailed from Callao, hoping to find the rich, legendary, great southern continent that had been postulated by geographers for many years. This was the first voyage to be made across the Pacific south of the equator. On Saturday, February 7, 1568, land so large and high was sighted that it was thought to be a continent. Mendaña had discovered the Solomon Islands but, after August 17, when he saw them sink beneath the horizon, they were not seen again by white men for two hundred years.

THE GREAT SOUTH SEA

It is not known who was responsible for naming the Solomons, but they were so called shortly after the ships returned to Mexico and tales of golden riches there grew into a legend. Mendaña must have begun to believe the legend himself for he was hankering to return to the Solomons, but it took him nearly thirty years to attempt to do so. Eventually he sailed once more from Callao, on April 9, 1595, with four ships and Pedro Fernandez de Quiros as pilot. On July 28 he sighted an island which he first thought was part of the Solomons. Actually he had discovered the Marquesas which he named in honor of the Marqués de Mendoza, Viceroy of Peru, and one of the sponsors of his voyage. Mendaña continued westward and discovered the Santa Cruz group where he died. The expedition was brought back by Quiros who ten years later led the third great Spanish expedition from the same Peruvian port. Proceeding on a more southerly course than on the previous voyage, he discovered some unidentifiable atolls in the Tuamotus, one of the Tokelau group, and the island of Espíritu Santo in the New Hebrides. Like Mendaña, when he saw the Solomons, Quiros thought Santa Cruz part of the great southern continent. His return to Mexico without making any further discoveries ended Spanish attempts at exploration in the Pacific.

If the sixteenth can be called the Spanish century of exploration, the seventeenth can certainly be called the Dutch. While the Spaniards were chasing golden legends over the horizon, the Hollanders were more interested in solid trade. Sailing from Holland on June 14, 1615, Willem Cornelis Schouten and Jakob Le Maire crossed to South America where one of their vessels was accidentally destroyed by fire. They continued with a single ship, found a passage between Tierra del Fuego and Staten Island which they called Le Maire Strait, and sailed around Cape Horn, naming it in honor of the city of Hoorn in Holland. Skirting the northern edge of the Tuamotus they discovered four islands and found two more in the Tongan group. Several other small islands, including Futuna, were discovered before they reached Batavia. Here, in their Javanese capital, the officials of the Dutch East India Company confiscated the vessel and arrested both leaders for trespassing on their monopoly. Schouten returned home, but Le Maire died on the voyage to Holland.

The second famous Dutch voyage was that of Abel Tasman, the first navigator to enter the Pacific from the west, who sailed from Batavia on August 14, 1642, and, rounding the southwest extremity of Australia, discovered Tasmania. He continued east, and sighted the high mountainous coast of New Zealand on December 13, where he was discouraged from landing when one of his boats was attacked by natives and three men were killed. Sailing on, he discovered more islands, passed through the Fijis, and returned to Batavia on June 15, 1643.

Seventy-nine years after Tasman the last Dutch expedition, commanded by Jacob Roggeveen, sailed on August 21, 1721, again in search of the great southern continent. Roggeveen entered the Pacific through Le Maire Strait, rounded the Horn, and sailed south until he reached ice. He turned north to Juan Fernández and, shifting his course westerly, discovered Easter Island on Sunday, April 6, 1722, and named it in honor of the day. Pushing westward, Roggeveen discovered six of the Tuamotus and the Manua group in eastern Samoa, sighted two other unidentified islands, and reached Java in September where his three ships, like that of Schouten and Le Maire, were confiscated.

The remaining eighteenth-century exploration was partly French and mostly English. In 1764 the British Admiralty sent out the frigate *Dolphin* and the sloop *Tamar* under the command of Commodore John Byron. Sailing June 21, Byron entered the Pacific through the Strait of Magellan, discovered a few small islands, and returned to England via the Cape of Good Hope. Byron had been sent into the Pacific to look for a western entrance to the Northwest Passage, but he was apparently so anxious to get home that he set a record for sailing around the world which was not equaled for some two hundred years.

Although the expedition was not especially successful, the Admiralty decided to send the *Dolphin* out once more under the command of Captain Samuel Wallis. She was accompanied by the sloop *Swallow* under Lieutenant Philip Carteret. The two vessels with a store ship sailed from Plymouth Sound, August 27, 1766. At the western end of the Strait of Magellan after a very difficult passage the *Dolphin* and *Swallow* parted company. Wallis navigated to the southward of Byron's track across the Pacific and, sailing through the middle of the Tuamotus, discovered half a dozen atolls before making his most famous discovery, June 18, 1767, when he reached Tahiti. He anchored in Matavai Bay, established friendly relations with the Tahitians, and, after recuperating for a month from the long sea voyage, the expedition pushed on to several other islands in the Society group. Wallis touched at Tinian and Batavia, and, after refitting at the Cape of Good Hope, arrived in The Downs on May 20, 1768.

It was thought that the *Swallow* had foundered but she survived the storm in which the two ships parted. Captain Carteret discovered Pitcairn Island, July 2, 1767, but, because of the rough sea, could not land. In the passage across the Pacific he discovered several smaller islands and finally arrived at Spithead, March 20, 1769, nearly a year after the return of the *Dolphin*.

NEW ENGLAND AND THE SOUTH SEAS

In January 1768, before Wallis arrived in Plymouth, a great French navigator Louis Antoine de Bougainville, who had served as an aide-de-camp to General Montcalm in Canada, entered the Pacific through the Strait of Magellan with his ships *Boudeuse* and *L'Etoile.* He sailed a westerly course between those followed by Byron and Wallis and discovered a new series of atolls in the Tuamotus. Arriving at Tahiti, April 2, he anchored on the opposite side of the island from Wallis' harbor, and stayed for a fortnight. Once more sailing west, he came to the same group of Samoan islands which Roggeveen had seen, and discovered the large island of Tutuila. Bougainville christened Samoa the Navigators' Islands, a name which they bore for many years. Later at the Cape of Good Hope he heard that Carteret had left the Cape Colony just three days before his arrival. Anxious to overtake his fellow circumnavigator he pushed on and sighted the *Swallow* on February 25, 1769. After he sincerely offered his services to the Englishman, the ships parted. Bougainville remarked: "His ship was very small, went very ill, and when we took leave of him, he remained as it were at anchor. How much he must have suffered in so bad a vessel may well be conceived." [1] Bougainville arrived at St. Malo on March 16, 1769.

When Wallis returned to England the Admiralty and the Royal Society were preparing another expedition for the primary purpose of observing the transit of the planet Venus. Lt. James Cook, who was appointed commander, had made a reputation for himself as a hydrographer in Newfoundland and the Gulf of St. Lawrence. He had first gone to sea on Whitby colliers and he selected a vessel of this type, the bark *Endeavour,* for the voyage. It was a fortunate choice for she was a far better ship for exploration than the naval vessels employed in the earlier expeditions. Cook, accompanied by Joseph Banks with a staff of naturalists and artists, sailed from Plymouth for Tahiti, in August, and rounded Cape Horn late in January. The blue mountains of Tahiti were sighted on April 10, 1769, and, after anchoring at Matavai Bay, an observatory was set up on Point Venus, where the transit was successfully observed under a clear sky. Cook then explored the remaining Windward Islands and discovered the Leeward group, which he named the Society Islands in honor of the Royal Society. After discovering Rurutu in the Australs, he continued on a southwest course until he reached the east coast of the north island

2. Papetoai Bay, Moorea

of New Zealand in the vicinity of Poverty Bay. Cook took six months to make a complete survey of the coasts of both the North and South Islands of New Zealand, and proved that they were separated by the strait now named for him. He also showed that they had no connection with Tasmania or the Great Southern Continent. After charting the east coast of Australia, Cook sailed to Batavia and returned to England via the Cape of Good Hope, anchoring in The Downs on July 13, 1771.

So rich was the result of this expedition that a second voyage was immediately prepared. This time it was proposed to prove once and for all whether or not a great southern continent existed. Cook sailed in 1772 with the ships *Resolution* and *Adventure,* the latter commanded by Captain Tobias Furneaux,

3. Tautira, Tahiti

and entered the Pacific from the west. Sailing south of Australia, he crossed to New Zealand and north to Tahiti. From there he visited the Tonga group, discovered a number of smaller islands, visited Easter Island and the Marquesas, and

THE GREAT SOUTH SEA

returned to Tahiti. After discovering Palmerston and Niue, he visited the New Hebrides, and New Zealand a second time, discovered New Caledonia and Norfolk Island, and pushed his search for the great southern continent down to Antarctica. By energetically exploring the ocean between New Zealand and Cape Horn he proved that no such continent existed. Cook returned through the South Atlantic, arriving at Spithead on July 30, 1775, after a voyage of three years and eighteen days.

After his second great circumnavigation Captain Cook was due for retirement, but he was persuaded to volunteer for a third voyage to settle another problem that had plagued geographers for centuries. Since Elizabethan days the English had been attempting to navigate the Northwest Passage and find a short cut to the wealth of the Indies through Arctic America. It was proposed that Cook should go into the Pacific and seek the western end of the passage. At the same time he was to return Omai, a Tahitian brought to England by Captain Furneaux, to his home in the Society Islands. The *Resolution* was refitted and another Whitby vessel, the *Discovery* under Captain Charles Clerke, made up the expedition. Once more the Pacific was entered via the Cape of Good Hope and, proceeding to the mid-Pacific, Cook discovered the Cook Islands, revisited Tonga and Tahiti, and discovered Tubuai in the Australs. As he sailed north to make his search for the passage, he discovered Christmas Island, and, on January 18, 1778, arrived at an unknown group which he named the Sandwich Islands for the Earl of Sandwich, First Lord of the Admiralty. He continued north through the Bering Strait until, stopped by the ice, he returned to winter in the Sandwich Islands. After being hospitably entertained by the chiefs at Kealakekua Bay in Hawaii, Cook sailed to continue his survey of the islands until a storm forced him to return for repairs. It was a tragic return, for Cook had outstayed his welcome and, in an altercation over a stolen boat, filled with misunderstandings on both sides, he was killed. The expedition proceeded under the command of Clerke and discovered the remaining Hawaiian Islands. Clerke too died, on the final search for the Northern

4. The King of Hawaii bringing presents to Captain Cook

Passage, and the expedition returned to England under the command of Captain John Gore (who was said to be a Virginian). The *Resolution* and *Discovery* anchored in the Nore, October 4, 1780, after a voyage of four years, two months and twenty-two days.

There was little left to discover in the Pacific after the voyages of Captain James Cook. He sailed farther, discovered more islands, surveyed more unknown coasts, and cleared up more geographical nonsense than any navigator before or since.

THE GREAT SOUTH SEA

And with Cook, New England's contact with the Pacific begins, for one of his marines was a Yankee.

John Ledyard was born in 1751 at Groton, Connecticut, on the banks of the Thames River opposite New London. His father, a sea captain who died at the age of thirty-five, had traded in the West Indies. At nineteen John was invited by the Reverend Eleazar Wheelock, an intimate friend of his grandfather, to enter Wheelock's new school at Hanover, New Hampshire. Ledyard went there in 1772, apparently intending to prepare for missionary work with the Indians.[2]

Ledyard's arrival at Hanover was spectacular. Driving a horse and dilapidated sulky from Hartford, he fetched the Dartmouth intervale in this unlikely rig, the first ever seen in the region. The journey could have been performed more easily on horseback, but the enterprising Ledyard would have had no room to carry his theatrical equipment; so he chose to navigate the heavily laden sulky through forest roads and across unbridged streams—no mean feat.

Ledyard's residence at Dartmouth lasted less than a year. He learned easily, but he was not a student and he was overly sensitive to criticism. After four months of college he vanished and is said to have wandered among the Six Nations Iroquois, returning in three and one-half months as nonchalantly as he left. His wanderlust carried him on countryside journeys and overnight mountain climbs until, bored with college, he persuaded some of his fellow students to help him cut down a great pine and from this they fashioned a dugout canoe fifty feet long. He left Hanover in Dr. Wheelock's absence and set off down the Connecticut River for Hartford, one hundred and forty miles away. Escaping catastrophe at Bellows Falls, Vermont, he safely completed this remarkable voyage through the wilderness and beached his canoe in front of his uncle's house one bright spring morning, where his astonished relatives saw him crawl out from under a bearskin and step ashore.

John Ledyard now decided, probably under his pious mother's influence, to study for the ministry with clergymen on Long Island. His theological studies were of even shorter duration than his college career, and shortly we find him as a sailor bound for the Mediterranean to fetch a cargo of mules to the West Indies. He jumped ship in Gibraltar and enlisted in the British Army; his captain found him strutting in full uniform and, not wanting to lose a sailor, persuaded him to return on shipboard after obtaining his release from the military.

When his ship returned to New London, Ledyard found himself at twenty-two, broke, out of work, and restless. He recalled tales of his grandfather's that the family had rich relatives in England, and decided to look them up. He shipped on a vessel bound for Plymouth, apparently worked his passage across, and walked begging his way to London where the son of the well-to-do English Ledyard personally gave him the cold shoulder.

Two forces now came to bear. Captain Cook, at the height of his fame, was preparing for his third voyage of exploration and the possibility of such a journey appealed to the young Yankee's wanderlust. Also he was destitute, so he enlisted in the marines. He volunteered for the Cook expedition, was made a corporal, and sailed for the South Seas on board the *Resolution,* July 12, 1776. *

Ledyard's request to be the official historian of the expedition after the death of Cook was refused; this desire was shared with every officer and scientist on the voyage. When the expedi-

---

* It was not unusual for Americans to serve in the British Navy before the Revolution. At the time Ledyard volunteered for Cook's voyage he did not know that the war had begun. After his return from the voyage, while on duty off New York, he deserted. He had no bitterness against the British Navy, but simply did not want to fight against his friends and neighbors.

tion returned his journal, like all others, was impounded until the official account could be published. This original journal has vanished.

After the return of Cook's ships, Ledyard remained in the Navy for two years, and in December 1782 arrived on a man-of-war in Long Island Sound. He obtained seven days' leave to visit his mother in Southold, Long Island, where she kept a boarding house frequented by British officers. After a surprise visit he went over "to the continent" as Sparks, his biographer, puts it, and deserted the British to return to his own country where he settled down in Hartford to write his account of Cook's voyage. The book, entitled *Journal of Captain Cook's Last Voyage to the Pacific Ocean and in Quest of a North West Passage, between Asia and America,* was published in Hartford 1783 and is now very rare. It was written between January 1 and May 1, 1783 and is based on a surreptitious account published in England before the official one and on Ledyard's own recollections. It contains some details not in other journals, including a version of Cook's death. More important Ledyard saw the possibility of a Northwest Coast fur trade with China. His remarks about the variety and richness of furs to be obtained there and his enthusiasm for the furs purchased for a trifle from the natives by Cook's sailors and sold in China at an enormous profit eventually had a great influence in New England. He says, "We purchased while here about 1500 beaver, besides other skins, but took none but the best, having no thoughts at that time of using them to any other advantage than converting them to the purposes of cloathing, but it afterwards happened that skins which did not cost the purchaser sixpence sterling sold in China for 100 dollars." [3]

After completing his book, Ledyard spent a year or more in an attempt to stimulate interest in a fur voyage to the Northwest Coast and thence to China. He interviewed various merchants along the Atlantic seaboard. The Philadelphia merchant Robert Morris was very interested in outfitting a ship for the purpose, but when the vessel was ready she was sent on a different voyage. Ledyard was equally unsuccessful in New York. He almost obtained the support of a close friend in New London, but his accounts were so glowing and his enthusiasm so extreme that he overdid it.

After a stay in Spain, Ledyard went to Paris where he met Thomas Jefferson, at that time Minister to the Court of France.

5. Early nineteenth-century traders on the Northwest Coast

His eagerness and knowledge aroused the interest of Jefferson who became quite enthusiastic over the possibility of the United States' developing the Northwest Coast fur trade. Also in Paris at this time was John Paul Jones on a mission from

Congress to straighten out the matter of certain prize money with the French. Ledyard and Jones were cut from the same bolt of cloth and they planned an elaborate expedition of two ships, to be sponsored if possible by the King of France, to go to the Northwest Coast for furs. It was planned that, after loading one ship, Ledyard would remain and collect furs for a second cargo while Jones went on to Canton, marketed his produce, and returned to the Northwest Coast. Jones would then take both ships to China, load with silks, teas, and products of that country, and go around the Cape of Good Hope to market the China goods. Ledyard planned to stay on the Northwest Coast to consolidate his position with the Indians and collect more furs. This scheme too was due for disappointment, and Ledyard never again saw the Pacific or the land of the rich furs or the wealth of China. After a walking expedition across Siberia, he went to Egypt where, seeking the sources of the Nile, he died in Cairo.

Ledyard is an important man in the history of American contacts in the South Seas. Not only was he the first New Englander in the Pacific, but he went there under the command of the great Captain Cook. He visualized in the most minute detail how the Northwest Coast–China trade should be carried out, and his ideas and enthusiasm undoubtedly influenced the eventual development of that trade.

If profits on furs first attracted Yankees into the Pacific, other economic resources of the vast region kept them coming there in increasing numbers. Sea otter skins dramatized the profits that enterprising men could make in the China market, but other sea and land furs of the Northwest Coast—beaver, ermine, fox, and seal, for example—brought excellent returns.

Good profits were also to be made on fur seal skins from the islands of South Atlantic, South Pacific, Antarctica, and western South America. Seal hunting, in fact, became a specialized activity and those who pursued it for the China market were a sharp, hard-bitten, and unscrupulous lot who followed their prey to the most remote and dangerous breeding grounds. Like their fellows on the Northwest Coast, however, it was not always possible to obtain full cargoes of pelts, particularly as the animals became depleted from overhunting. Then both fur traders and sealers, as they crossed the Pacific, searched for other merchandise to round out their cargoes and the Pacific Islands provided such products.

Sandalwood, which the Chinese had previously obtained mostly from India, was found growing in the Hawaiian Islands, Fiji, and elsewhere. The reefs of the Fiji Islands, especially, also supplied tons of the sea slug, known when cured as trepang or *bêche-de-mer,* relished by the Chinese as soup. Both sandalwood and bêche-de-mer trades developed into specialties. Lesser but still important South Sea harvests in tortoise shell, pearl shell, pearls, and edible birds' nests also produced satisfactory profits in the Manila or Canton markets. While a captain might specialize in one trade, frequently full cargoes of a single product were unobtainable and he was forced to collect a mixed bag. This became more common as the wealth of original resources declined. To facilitate filling ships promptly, Yankees set up trading establishments in New Zealand, Fiji, the Northwest Coast, and above all the Hawaiian Islands, where they imported trade goods for the natives, kept ships' stores on hand, and collected cargoes for the vessels.

One of the greatest single economic resources of the Pacific, which had nothing to do with the China trade, was the sperm whale or cachalot. This ubiquitous creature roams all the world's oceans but was found more abundantly than elsewhere on certain grounds of the temperate and tropical Pacific.

THE GREAT SOUTH SEA

Here was the best oil supply to light homes and provide one of New England's most important exports; up until the Civil War, whaling in the Pacific and the supplying of whaleships was big business. Because of the long duration of their voyages, the whalers, depended upon the Pacific Islands for fresh supplies of food, water, and wood and for recreation.

The products that originally brought the enterprising Yankees to the Pacific, some of the highest valued natural resources of their day, were far different from the present economic products of the region. Sea otters, sandalwood, and whales have been depleted and the markets have changed; today, copra, sugar, vanilla, pineapples, nitrate, and phosphate are the main products. But the earlier trade stabilized the contacts and often laid the basis for the later ones. So, too, it laid the foundations for the introduction of Christianity, for where the hand of Mammon falls the hand of God usually follows, and for the international rivalries and political influences of the great powers during the past century.

II ~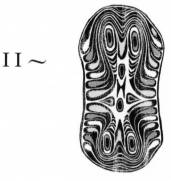

HUNTING THE CACHALOT

The whale fishery in America began very soon after the first settlement of New England, but gradually it diminished north of Cape Cod and in the eighteenth and early nineteenth centuries it became concentrated on the island of Nantucket. By the second quarter of the nineteenth century the industry was dominated by New Bedford, although New London, Connecticut, and Sag Harbor, Long Island, were also important whaling ports. The Nantucketers developed a system of whaling far more efficient than that employed by the English, Dutch, or Basques who were the principal whalers of Europe. It had been the custom in the European industry to bring the blubber home in casks and try it out after the ship returned to her home port. When Nantucket men began going farther offshore, however, they discovered sperm whales in the warm waters of the Gulf Stream. The increased distance from home and the warm climate were undoubtedly influences in the invention of tryworks aboard ship, which it soon became obvious was a far more efficient method.

As in any specialized industry, whaling equipment, from ships down to the smallest tools, was of a singular nature developed by trial and error until each thing was the most efficient for its particular purpose. No seaman would ever confuse a trim merchant vessel with the bluff-bowed, sturdily built whaler whose speed was of little consequence. They were good, weather ships but poor sailers. Melville's comment on one whaler, that she could not sail faster than "you could whip a toad through tar," applied to most of them. And if they were slow to begin with, they were even slower after a two- to four-year cruise, slogging their way homeward deep laden, the holds filled with oil and with yards of weed growing on their bottoms. The whaler was built to maintain herself at sea for up to four years, and she could be mistaken for nothing else as she cruised about under shortened sail, reeking of oil, her whale boats high on the big wooden davits ready to fall at the first alarm, her trypots smoking—weather-beaten, homely, efficient. The ship, square-rigged on three masts, was commonly used in the early nineteenth century, but the bark with its fore-and-aft mizzen mast became favored in the later heyday of whaling. Those vessels first in the Pacific were small, but size increased as the voyages became longer. The *Beaver* of Nantucket measured only 240 tons, and together with cargo cost a little over $10,000. Fifty years later ships ranged from 300 to 500 tons and cost from $30,000 to $60,000. Unless lost by storm or accident they cruised the seas for years.

Although the ships were ugly but efficient, the whaleboats (most ships normally carried four on davits and two spares) were the most graceful and finest pulling boats ever built. Twenty-eight to thirty feet long, double-ended, sleek, and buoyant, they were rowed by five oars with a steersman. The forward rower was also the harpooner and, after he had sunk his iron in a whale, he and the mate, who held the steering oar, changed places and the latter drove his lance to the kill. Men, oars, paddles, mast and sails, lines, harpoons, lances, and other gear were arranged and stowed in the most precise and scientific manner in these small craft for the slightest error could mean a stove boat or death.

Whaling was a conservative occupation and changed only slowly over the years. In the later days the captain seldom left his ship for the hunt but earlier he was the first to lower and the ship was left in charge of a ship keeper. Toggle harpoons replaced fluke harpoons, bomb lances replaced hand lances, and eventually the bomb harpoon, which made fast to the whale and killed at the same time, evolved.

When whales were sighted one or more boats were lowered and the pursuit began. On approaching within three fathoms of the whale, the officer ordered "stand up," whereupon the harpooner dropped his oar and took his place in the bow with the harpoon which he darted into the whale as soon as the boat was on. If there was time he also threw the second harpoon and the officer ordered, "stern all," backing the boat off to get clear of the whale's flurry. After a boat was fast to a whale the beast might run, giving an exciting "Nantucket sleigh ride," or sound; if he went too deep the line had to be cut to prevent the boat from being carried under. After a whale was killed it was brought alongside the ship, the blubber stripped off and tryed out, the oil sealed in casks, the whalebone collected, and if the prey was sperm, the case bailed out, and the carcass turned adrift. The hunt continued until the ship was full or supplies were so diminished that home port was made again.

Nantucket with its poor soil and scanty resources became a one-industry island. The people's livelihood was from the

HUNTING THE CACHALOT

sea and, as the old Nantucket proverb says, "there is the green pasture where our children's children will go for their bread." Sailors from this seagirt sand pile ranged the Atlantic from the Arctic Circle to the far south, from the Americas to Africa, hunting down their prey with a determination and efficiency never known before. Neither colonial troubles with British regulations relating to whaling in the north nor various complications with English and French tariffs deterred the islanders. If Nantucketers could not sail on local ships they became captains of British whalers; William Rotch even based his fleet at Dunkirk, France.

As the demand for whale oil increased, so did the fleets of ships, and the numbers of men employed in the industry. As the whales were fished out in near grounds, the ships pushed farther and farther into the most remote parts of the sea; but, until the late eighteenth century no whaler had penetrated into the Pacific.

During the War of 1812 whaling along with all other maritime activities went into a decline. Some ships were out in the Pacific but the sailings and returns were few. After the war New Bedford with its deep harbor rose quickly to leadership in the whaling field and became a greater port than Nantucket had even been. The bar at Nantucket made it impossible for larger ships to come in loaded unless they were carried over it by the ingenious "camel," a device which lifted vessels just enough to carry them across the shallow water. Thus, during the middle of the nineteenth century New Bedford with larger ships of three to five hundred tons dominated the field, and the bark rig became the most popular for whaling activities. The British, too, were exploiting the rich Pacific whaling grounds, but gradually the men from Buzzards Bay and Long Island Sound fished them off the ocean.

NEW ENGLAND AND THE SOUTH SEAS

✳

Luring the whaleman into the Pacific was first and fore-most the sperm whale or cachalot, as it was known to the French. This great beast, which sometimes reached over eighty feet in length, produced the finest grade of oil; in its ponderous head, which monopolized almost a third of the creature's length, was the natural cavity from which the pure case oil, most valuable of all, was bailed. Immediately below the case in the front part of the head was the section known as "junk" which produced the finest spermaceti, spongy and without odor, for candles and ointments. In its long lower jaw grew the large white teeth beloved by the scrimshander, a valuable arti-cle to swap for fresh provisions to island natives or traders. Sperm provided year-round whaling, mostly between latitudes 40° north and 40° south with seasonal migrations between the northern and southern limits of its range or at least from its extremities toward the equator.

Slightly more than half of the Pacific catch was made up of the somewhat less profitable toothless or whalebone whales. The right whale overlapped the territory of the sperm in the Sea of Japan, but in general there were few of these creatures between 30° north and 30° south. In the Coral Sea, off the northwestern shores of Australia, off New Caledonia, and around the Tonga Islands roamed the humpback, now nearly extinct, while beyond 53° north and through the Bering Strait into the Arctic cruised the great northern whale or bowhead. The California gray whale was the object of the shore-based lagoon whaling off Southern California where they gamboled among the shoals and in the breakers on their southward migration from the Arctic.

Besides oil, all of these whales produced the baleen for

corset stays, umbrellas, buggy whips, and other uses. Oil as well as skins was also obtained from sea elephants (the largest males may be over twenty feet long) which inhabited the California coast and the remote islands of the Southern Hemisphere, especially Kerguelen and the Herds, in enormous numbers.

6. Ship *South Carolina* sperm whaling

A factor other than the vast quantities of sperm whales made the Pacific a pleasanter ocean for whaling than the empty Atlantic. Throughout the Pacific there are thousands of islands where a ship long at sea could stop to refresh the crew and obtain fresh vegetables, fruit, and clean water. These were inhabited by races of natives who more often than not welcomed the diversions which the visitors provided. The American whaleman was no saint and often there were fights, needless slaughter, and massacres. Disease introduced spread

NEW ENGLAND AND THE SOUTH SEAS

rapidly and with deadly effect, especially in the palm-covered coral atolls and the high volcanic paradises of Polynesia. But there were dangers to the whaleman that he did not have to contend with in the Atlantic, for if the seas were longer and easier, the ocean more clement after the grueling beat around the Horn, there lurked beneath those blue waters some of the most dangerous coral reefs to be found anywhere in the world.

Unlike merchant ships, whalers had few real sailors in their crews. Most sailors looked down on the vessels as stinkpots. Consequently, the owners, hard put to man their vessels, maintained shipping offices in inland cities for the recruiting of seamen. As the old whaling song begins:

> 'Tis advertised in Boston, New York and Buffalo,
> Five hundred brave Americans, a whaling for to go,
>   Singing, Blow, ye winds in the morning,
>   And blow ye winds, high-o!
>   Clear away your running gear,
>   And blow, ye winds high-o![1]

Agents combed the hinterlands of New England and New York state to lure adventurous farm boys to ship on a whaler. The life was pictured as easy and glamorous and agents outdid themselves in outrageously misinterpreting it. Samuel Eliot Morison remarks, "A well-known Boston agent, after describing to a Maine plough boy the imaginary joys of this glorious profession, concluded confidentially, 'Now, Hiram, I'll be *honest* with yer. When yer out in the boats chasin' whales, yer git yer mince-pie *cold*.'"[2] Besides the farm boys there was a sprinkling of derelicts swept out of the waterfront boarding houses and grogshops, another sprinkling of Indians largely from Gay Head on Martha's Vineyard, as well as Negroes and South Sea Islanders. As the century wore on, more and more men known as Bravas, from the Azores and Canary Islands, were employed, and there was a scattering of nearly every other nationality. At the beginning of a voyage the green hands were broken in by hardened mates, the old hands sobered up, and the boat crews whipped into efficient teams. Whaling in reality had little romance. It was a rough, tough, dirty business even at best under a humane captain; under one who was not, a whaler could become a hellship.

The length and uncertainty of the voyage together with the lay system of pay kept the number of real sailors in the whaling service at a minimum. Whalemen from captain down to boys were paid, not by time or take, but on a fraction of the net earnings of the voyage specified and arrived at through owner's policy, individual bargaining, skill and experience of the employee, duration of the voyage, and other factors. It was flexible and ranged from as high as ⅛ for a top-notch captain to as little as ⅓₅₀ for a boy. The sailor's living was included, excepting for clothing and bedding which was charged against his lay. Any other advances or debts were charged; and the lay could not be figured until the end of the voyage when the cargo was appraised at the current prices for oil and bone. Officers and harpooners received a sufficiently large lay to get a decent return for their voyage, but the seaman often found himself making a two- or three-year voyage for barely nothing, if not actually in debt to the owners.

Large crews cramped in close quarters required stern discipline, and floggings were not uncommon. Forecastles were dirty and vermin-ridden. The air was stagnant with the sickening smells of bilge, oil, and unwashed men. Monotony alternated with periods of driving, exhausting work. Food, although plentiful, was cheap, uninspired, and, frequently, toward the end of a voyage, revolting. Little wonder that, when the whalers came into the Pacific and stopped at tropical islands that were nearer to paradise than any of the weary whalemen could possibly imagine, many of the crew jumped ship. In the nineteenth century the Pacific islands were swarming with renegade white men, many of them New England sailors who took native mistresses and raised large families. Escaped convicts from Australia, along with other lawless elements that drifted into the Pacific during the early and

7. The South Sea whale fishery

middle nineteenth century, turned the islands into one of the most ungoverned regions on earth.

While it was the English whaler *Amelia,* owned by the London firm of Enderby and Sons that first penetrated the Pacific in 1789, both her captain and first mate were from Nantucket. So was Archaelus Hammond, later himself a captain, a crew member who became the first man to kill a sperm whale in the Pacific. When the *Amelia* returned around

HUNTING THE CACHALOT

the Horn in 1790 with a full cargo of oil, the result of the voyage was catalytic in whaling circles. There was feverish activity in Nantucket to exploit the new rich grounds. In 1791 four Nantucket ships, mostly new vessels, and one, the *Rebecca,* from New Bedford rounded the Horn to the onshore whaling grounds near the Peruvian coast. Captain Paul Wirth in the *Beaver* of Nantucket is generally recognized as being the first American whaler in the Pacific, although that honor has been disputed by the *Rebecca.* Certain it is that *Rebecca,* arriving at New Bedford on February 23, 1793, was the first to return from the Pacific to an American port with a cargo of oil. The *Washington,* another Nantucket vessel that sailed the same year, is noted as the first American ship to show our flag in a Spanish Pacific port when Captain George Bunker took her into Callao for provisions in July of 1792.

Once the Horn was rounded whalers went there in increasing numbers and spread throughout the Pacific as they had swarmed through the Atlantic before. Certain areas were found to be particularly good hunting grounds. The waters around the Juan Fernández Islands off the coast of Chile, together with the onshore grounds along the coast of Peru, were the first frequented. The rich offshore grounds, between 100° and 140° west, near the equator, were known as the on-the-line grounds. Another good area was in the waters among the Gilbert Islands. The South Pacific also provided good "fishing," as it was called, around Fiji and north of New Zealand. During the Southern Hemisphere's summer there were whales in abundance on the middle ground between New Zealand and Australia, but in the opposite season the whales were thickest in the Northern Hemisphere on the "Japan grounds."

American whalers entered the Pacific by way of both Cape Horn and the Cape of Good Hope. From the time whaling became common in the Pacific until 1840, when the British established sovereignty over New Zealand, the most popular place for the whalers to refit was the Bay of Islands near the northern end of the North Island of New Zealand. The place had many advantages—good bold water close to shore in protected anchorages and ample supplies of timber for firewood as well as masts and spars. The supply of pure water was ample also, and fruit, fresh vegetables, and meat could be obtained in plenty. The usual meat bought at the Bay of Islands was pork, for swine were introduced there by Governor King of New South Wales in 1793, although Captain Cook on his second and third voyages in 1773 and 1778 had left breeding stock of hogs and goats on the South Island. By 1805 the Maoris, as the New Zealand natives are called, had many acres of land under cultivation and were doing a thriving business with the whalers and traders. Charles Darwin on the voyage of the *Beagle* described the port in his diary on December 21, 1835, as follows:

Early in the morning we entered the Bay of Islands, . . . The country is hilly, but with a smooth outline; and it is deeply intersected by numerous arms, extending from the bay. The surface appears from a distance, as if clothed with coarse pasture, but this in truth is nothing but fern. On the more distant hills, as well as in patches in some of the valleys, there is a good deal of wood-land. The general tint of the landscape is not a bright green; and it resembles the country a short distance to the southward of Concepcion in Chile. In several parts of the bay, little villages of square tidy-looking houses were scattered close down to the waters edge. Three whaling ships were lying at anchor; but with the exception of these, and of a few canoes now and then crossing from one shore to the other, an air of extreme quietness reigned over the whole district.[3]

HUNTING THE CACHALOT

To obtain necessary supplies the white man, whaler and trader alike, brought with him tobacco and trinkets, and, what was worse, firearms and rum. The result on the Polynesians was disastrous. No real single village or settlement existed at Bay of Islands before 1814, but late that year the Reverend Samuel Marsden after a preliminary visit preached his first sermon to the Maoris and organized the first mission of the Church Missionary Society. As the settlement grew more white men moved in. Besides the missionaries a group of shop owners and traders grew up and the number of convicts from Australia and deserters from ships increased, many of them "going native" to live in the bush. The trade, too, increased, and the Maoris began to demand more cloth and blankets, more tools and fish hooks, in addition to firearms and liquor, for their vegetables, meat, and tattooed heads. With this increasing population of convicts, runaway sailors, honest craftsmen, both honest and dishonest traders, half-castes, missionaries, and natives, there was absolutely no legal government. Great Britain seemed to have no interest whatsoever, although Captain Cook had taken possession of New Zealand in the name of George III in 1769. John B. Knights of Salem, who was there as master of the brig *Spy,* a trading vessel, in 1833 divided all of the white inhabitants into two groups—first, missionaries and adventurers, and, second, bare-faced villains. He thought little of either group and after paying his respects to the first, remarked, "The other class are far less to be feared because they act in character and seem, what they in reality are." [4]

By 1840, when the British government did take over, the Bay of Islands was the principal rendezvous for whalers' "wooding and watering" in the South Pacific, and whalers from the United States exceeded in number those of all other countries combined. In the six months previous to July 30,

1839, thirty-seven American whalers, mostly from Nantucket, New Bedford, and Warren, Rhode Island, came into the Bay of Islands. The traders and natives were doing a rushing business. The Maoris specialized in catching sailors who tried to run away for, as Robert Coffin of the *Logan* tells, "Several of the boys tried to run away, but the Maories caught them, tied their feet and hands together, slung them on poles, and brought them back after a reward was offered." 5

The size and activity of the whaling fleet were the envy of the English. Edmond Burke paid tribute to American energy when he remarked, "No sea, but what is vexed by their fisheries—no climate that is not witness of their toils." 6 Besides the whalers increasing numbers of trading vessels from New England were coming into the Bay of Islands, and it became necessary for the United States government to establish a consulate there. The first American Consul was an Englishman, but the second was John B. Williams of Salem, who was living at the Bay of Islands as a trader. Williams castigates the white population in his journal. He remarks, "European diseases have been introduced and the natives are easy victims. They have begun to depopulate and degenerate very fast. From 1818 to 1839 it is estimated that more than one half of some tribes have died of disease." And, he continues: "When a ship arrives her decks are almost instantly lined with native women —a floating castle of prostitution. How can it be different when the Master and Officers set the example. . . . Mischief and misery have been reduced to a system." Of the liberal flow of liquor, "Drunkenness is also the curse of the Bay of Islands and this is largely European drunkenness. Even on temperance whaling ships, once ashore the men entered into drunkenness. When drunk sailors break the ships' articles and the vessel is forced to remain until the crew is replenished. The pugnacity of these drunks is terrific." [7] Such a situation created largely by the whalers, was a source of constant embarrassment to the missionaries and increased their labors a hundredfold. But labor on they did, and in the end, aided by some honest, resident white men and a sober element among the seamen, their teachings and example made headway.

There is no doubt that the Bay of Islands needed law and order and, when Captain William Hobson, R.N., arrived in January 1840 and read the royal proclamation by which New Zealand became a part of New South Wales, it was a first step toward ending the chaotic conditions. But, while there is no doubt the port needed discipline, the establishment of a British Colony did not work for the good of American interests. Port duties and excise taxes were instituted at once. No longer could whale oil be landed for transshipping at very little cost. In addition to port charges, there was a duty of from 10 to 500 percent on all American articles brought in for trade. Timber and timberlands became the exclusive right of the Crown, and the expense of ship repairs was greatly increased. Business was driven away and the natives and traders longed for the good old lawless days. It was planned that the settlement at the Bay of Islands should be the capital city of the new colony, and it was named Russell in honor of Lord John Russell. (It was informally called Hobson's Folly when the governor's cow fell and broke its neck.) With business gone, the place was impractical; shortly thereafter the capital was relocated at Auckland.

While port charges and tonnage duties drove the Americans out of the Bay of Islands in 1840, they already had another string to their bow. As early as the 1820's New England whale ships had been visiting the Hawaiian ports of Honolulu, Lahaina, and Hilo for the same purposes as they visited the Bay of Islands. These ports had another advantage for, as the whalers depleted the whales in the warm waters of the Pacific, they were forced to move farther and farther north, eventually penetrating through Bering Strait and into the Arctic whaling grounds.

Not only were the New England whalers hunting the sperm whale off the seas, they were also putting the English and other European whalers out of business. One Englishman who seemed to know the circumstances in both the English and American whaling fleets wrote an unsigned letter to the *London Times* which was printed 9 June 1846. American whalemen were generally considered an unruly lot, but he considered his compatriots even worse.

SOUTH SEA WHALERS

Sir,—In your valuable paper of this date, you have an interesting article on the whale fishery of the Americans. I have served with the vessels of that country for a period of nearly six years, and am particularly acquainted with the details of this hazardous occupation. You seem to be surprised that the English whalers should have fallen off, whilst those of the Americans should have increased. A few words will explain it, —the greater cost of fitting out whalers here, the drunkenness, incapacity, and want of energy of the masters and crews. I have known English whalers to be out four years and take 1,300 or 1,400 barrels of oil, and American vessels cruising almost on the same "ground" would probably have captured twice as much. It would not interest you or your readers, were I to enter into the details of the difference in the *modus operandi* of English and American whalers. In the one there is order, obedience, energy, temperance; in the other, generally want of discipline, drunkenness, and incapacity to take whales when they do see them. One need not be surprised at the result. But the object and purport of my addressing you is to give you as near as I can calculate the number of foreigners employed in the American whale trade. I am practically acquainted with the subject, for I have made it a study.

He goes on to say that a fifth are of British extraction, another fifth are Portuguese from the Western or Cape Verde Islands, and three-fifths are American seamen. He continues:

There are upwards of 11,000 of American seamen in the service, inured to every danger and to the extremes of hardship and toil. These men think lightly of lowering boats after whales, the ship being at the time unable to carry a single reefed topsail.

I have little sympathy for the Americans, for as a body, I do not believe you could well find a more dishonest people, but their energy in bringing the trade to the pitch it has arrived at, deserves the highest encomium. Ten years since, "Honolulu," the capital of "Oahu," one of the Sandwich Islands, was a small insignificant village; it is now a flourishing town, with streets, dock-yards, and stores, and all this has been done by the American whalemen. The north-west fleet generally recruit at "Maui," (another of the Sandwich Islands) and the merchants at "Oahu" take goods and bills of exchange in return for the supplies which are furnished to the ships through them. Two or three hundred of the whalemen are annually supplied from these islands with everything they require, and the goods and money which they circulate in the island have caused the present prosperity. If ever a war should break out with America, our Government, it is hoped, will pounce upon these whalemen.[8]

8. Rotch's whalers in a shoal of sperm whales off Hawaii

NEW ENGLAND AND THE SOUTH SEAS

The dominance of American whaling is shown by the fact that in 1843 out of 140 whaling vessels arriving at the Hawaiian Islands, 132 were American. In 1844, 160 whaling vessels visited Honolulu and 326 whalers arrived at the port of Lahaina; in all 434 whale ships visited the Hawaiian Islands that year. The Islands received a further increase in visiting whale ships upon the discovery of the rich whaling grounds off the coast of Japan, and Honolulu reached its peak as a whaling rendezvous between 1850 and the Civil War. Whalers crowded its harbor twice yearly: in March preparing for the north, and during the last two months of the year fitting out for sperm in warmer waters.

The first whaler to enter the port of Honolulu was the *Mary,* under Captain Joseph Allen, which arrived in 1820; she was soon followed by many others. Rather ironically, 1820 is the same year in which the first party of missionaries arrived under the Reverend Hiram Bingham on the brig *Thaddeus.* The year before, however, the ship *Balena* of New Bedford, Captain Edmund Gardner, had put in at Kealakekua Bay. Supplying the enormous fleet of whale ships that put in at the Hawaiian Islands became one of the principal businesses. Mark Twain, who visited the islands in 1866, wrote prophetically: "The Whaling trade of the North Seas centers in Honolulu. Shorn of it, this town would die . . . though this town might flourish afterwards as a fine sugar plantation." [9] So important did the base become that Honolulu itself became a whaling port. Many of the ships from Nantucket and New Bedford sailed out of Honolulu continually and the oil was transshipped back to New England.

The Hawaiian Islands were an ideal place for the whalers to refit and as a base of operations in the Pacific; it was also an excellent place for crews to desert and a source of mutinies.

HUNTING THE CACHALOT

The shipowners of Nantucket, worried about conditions there, presented several memorials to the President of the United States complaining of conditions which endangered their investments. They feared that the Islands would become a nest of pirates and murderers and requested protection, for they said that nearly a hundred whale ships visited the islands every year and as many were lying in the port of Honolulu at one time.

To allay this situation Captain Thomas Ap Catesby Jones, commanding the United States sloop-of-war *Peacock,* was sent to the islands. He arrived at Honolulu in October 1826, and stayed for three months. He first turned his attention to ridding the islands of American runaway sailors, and, secondly, took up the claims of American traders against the Hawaiian king and chiefs. The presence of the sloop-of-war gave somewhat more stability to social conditions in the port.

9. Papeete Harbor, Tahiti

While there is no doubt that the whalers were an undisciplined, tough lot, difficult to control when on shore leave, there is another point of view. That side is shown by the Reverend Daniel Wheeler who visited Tahiti in 1835 and complained about many whalers there. He says that on May 15 of that year there were six American whalers, one trading vessel, and one English whaler, all large and well-manned, lying in Tahiti.[10] Wheeler distributed tracts to the sailors and dined with some of the whaling captains. Apparently most of them were sympathetic and many of the Nantucket and New Bedford men, who were Quakers, sailed what were known as "temperance ships." Wheeler says:

> We have met with great civility and willingness to lend a helping hand in many of the American captains: at the same time we are frequently sensible of a mixture which cannot be reconciled. The foregoing remark has no allusion to the inconsistent conduct of the crews of many of the American vessels, which we have fallen in with here, that are called "temperance ships."

He goes on to say that these he views with satisfaction, but that he discovers

> with horror and surprise, that the word temperance applies only to the ships, and not to their crews, none probably of which are members of a Temperance Society, but are merely bound by articles that the voyage shall be performed without any spirits being on board, except as medicine, if needed, and that their sobriety only exists because they cannot get the liquor; when on shore, and unbound by these articles, they are lamentably, in many instances, notorious for drinking to excess; and their immoral conduct, at this place, makes me shudder for the awful and woeful consequences, both as regards themselves, and the daughters of Tahiti.[11]

On July 16, 1835, the ship *Charles Carroll*, Captain Reuben Weeks of Rhode Island, arrived twenty months out and stayed at Tahiti for some days. Weeks was quite sympathetic with the missionaries and invited them to hold a meeting on board his ship. Wheeler thought that was a fine idea, provided the entire crew should be present of their own free will. He says,

> I had no objection to the meeting being held on board the *Charles Carroll,* provided the whole crew, without any compulsory measures being adopted, should be found willing to attend it, but that they should be left at their liberty to choose for themselves in this matter. It is a regular custom, on board whaling ships, when lying here, to allow one half of the seamen to be daily on shore for exercise; and therefore I am desirous that all who may attend our meeting should do it of their own accord, as it was known that only one half of the ship's company attended our meeting last *first day,* the other half having claimed the privilege of their liberty. As this doubt was removed to my satisfaction, the meeting was appointed to be held, as proposed, at eleven o'clock to-morrow morning.[12]

It would be interesting to know what means Captain Weeks employed to keep the entire crew on board for the occasion, but the service was held as scheduled with everyone present. Wheeler also tells that, although spirits were not used on board these temperance ships, scarcely one arrived which did not have rum, muskets, and gunpowder for sale to the natives. "These articles are brought in great abundance, particularly by the American ships, many of which are styled temperance ships" and "it is an absolute fact incontrovertible that vessels of this description have landed larger quantities of spirits on some islands than any other class of ships. On almost every island the population decreases and the dreadful ravages made by disease is much aggravated by the use of spirits." [13] The island of Bora Bora he tells us has suffered the most in the Society Islands.*

A continual scattering of impecunious whalers became bums and beachcombers in the South Seas. Some were deserters, some obtained discharges, and others were left behind

---

* This is interesting for I spent three weeks on Bora Bora in 1957, and found the people for the most part healthy, robust, and happy, even after having had their small island occupied for several years during World War II by the American military.

NEW ENGLAND AND THE SOUTH SEAS

by unscrupulous captains, usually near the end of a voyage, for their lays. Wilkes writes:

Many Americans are found on the different islands, who have been turned ashore from whale-ships, or left because they have broken their liberty a single time, near the end of a voyage. Such treatment leaves too much ground to believe that they are purposely left, in order to increase the profits of the ship-master or owners. Several of these men were received, in a perfectly destitute condition, on board the *Vincennes.* [14]

To fill out crews made thin by desertions, South Sea islanders, generally known as Kanakas, were numbered among most whaling crews in the Pacific. New Zealand Maoris, Marquesans, Tahitians, and others were employed, but the friendly Hawaiians were most numerous. It is estimated that between five and six hundred of these were sailing aboard American whalers in 1844 alone. And, although a captain had to post a bond which was forfeited unless he returned a Kanaka to his native island within three years, it was a regulation cavalierly regarded.

The impact of whalers on the South Sea Islands was tumultuous and many of the scars left were permanent. But if they were hard on the native peoples they were also hard on themselves. Mutiny was by no means uncommon. Sometimes natives forced on board mutinied against the few white men left when most of the crews were out in the boats chasing whales; at other times white crews rose against their officers. The best known and probably the most shocking mutiny occurred on the whale ship *Globe* of Nantucket in 1824. The *Globe,* under the command of Captain Thomas Worth of Martha's Vineyard, had sailed in December 1822. A year later, after cruising on the Japan ground, she returned to Oahu. Here some of her crew deserted and six new hands were shipped. At the end of December she sailed again, and a month later, on January 25, 1824, Samuel B. Comstock, one of her boat steerers, with four others of her crew crept into the cabin. Comstock killed Captain Worth with an ax, and the other ringleader of the mutineers, Samuel Payne, stabbed the first mate. They then broke into the stateroom of the second mate, John Lombard, and third mate, Nathaniel Fisher. After a fierce struggle Lombard was stabbed with a bayonet and Fisher shot through the head by Comstock. The bodies of the officers were thrown overboard and the mutineers took the ship to the Mulgrave Islands in the eastern Marshalls. Here, after a dispute among themselves, Payne murdered Comstock and the natives attacked the other mutineers and killed all but two. These men, after living on the island as captives for two years, were finally rescued by Captain John ("Mad Jack") Percival in the U.S.S. *Dolphin.* (Before the attack of the natives on the mutineers, however, Gilbert Smith, another boat steerer, with five of the crew who had not taken part in the mutiny, escaped to the ship and sailed her to Valparaiso where they arrived June 7, 1824. Among those who survived were George Comstock, a sixteen-year-old younger brother of the mutineers' ringleader.)

About twenty-five years later an equally brutal mutiny began on the New Bedford whaler *Junior* on Christmas Eve, 1857. Twenty-seven-year-old Archibald Mellon, Jr., of Nantucket was her captain; his first mate was Nelson Provost of New Bedford. Another New Bedford veteran, Nelson T. Lord, was second mate, and John Smith of Boston was the third officer. Provost was apparently a real bucko and treated his hands with inexcusable cruelty. Working himself into a fury, he would kick, knock, and curse them. The food, at first adequate, became moldy and wormy, a fact which the cook tried to conceal by mixing the crawling bread with grease and frying it as scouse for breakfast. One of the seamen declared, "We could eat wormy bread" but not the scouse because, "sometimes there would be half a dozen worms in a cake and sometimes more." Again one of the boat steerers was the leader. Cyrus Plummer, an unstable individual of mysterious past, after originally planning with some of the crew to jump ship at the first opportunity, began to consider a mutiny and seizure of the *Junior*. The ship had been at sea six months without sighting a whale and had cast anchor to celebrate the Christmas holiday. The food was no better, but about six o'clock in the afternoon of Christmas day the Captain gave a small glass of brandy to each of the men and the second mate gave Plummer a bottle of gin to distribute. Everyone except the watch then retired for the night. Apparently fortified with Dutch courage, Plummer, around midnight, said, "By God this thing must be done tonight"; when a sailor asked what, he replied, "Take the ship." On the morning of the 26th Plummer and four of the crew crept into the officers' cabin with loaded guns and fired at the four officers simultaneously. The wounded first mate was promised his life if he would navigate the vessel until they were in sight of land. On January 4, the mutineers were landed near Cape Howe, Australia, after extracting a promise from Provost that he would head the ship toward New Zealand, which would give the rascals time to lose themselves in the hinterland. Provost, instead of going to New Zealand, headed for Sydney, where he reported the affair to the authorities. The mutineers were promptly caught and sent back to New Bedford to stand trial. The case dragged through the courts and through two trials for the deplorable conditions aboard the ship were taken into consideration. Eventually Plummer was hanged and three of the others were convicted of manslaughter, receiving two years and ten months of hard labor.[15]

The destruction of boats by whales was not uncommon, but that the ultimate in disaster—the destruction of the whale

HUNTING THE CACHALOT

ship itself by the monster—was not unknown is demonstrated by the well-known incident of the *Essex* of Nantucket. On November 20, 1819, she was rammed and sunk by an infuriated sperm just south of the equator in 119° west longitude. Those of the ship's company who survived did so only after suffering the most excruciating hunger and exposure and resorting to cannibalism.

One of the constant, if unspectacular, perils in tropical waters, particularly to whale ships at sea for long periods, was the ship worm or teredo. Copper bottoming protected hulls from the creatures, but once they found a way to get into the planking they could be deadly, and there was no way of knowing that they were there. An example of their insidious work is provided by the ship *Minerva* of New Bedford, under the command of Captain Swain. While cruising in the Gilbert Islands in August 1856, the *Minerva* touched lightly on a reef. There was little wind, the sea was smooth, and no obvious damage resulted. The voyage continued, but during a heavy blow the following March the ship began to leak. The leaking continued until by the end of March she was making about sixteen inches of water an hour, requiring a backbreaking 2400 strokes per hour on the pumps to keep her clear. When the fore hold was cleared in an attempt to locate the trouble, several holes were disclosed through which the water was rushing in. These were plugged with canvas and blankets weighted down by anchor chains, but the pumps still had to work twenty-four hours a day. When the *Minerva* arrived in Sydney on April 7, Captain Swain had her hauled out for examination. She had lost two sheets of copper, probably on the Gilbert Islands reef. Where the planks were exposed the teredo had eaten them to a shell and it was a miracle that they had held together under the pressure of the plugging.

The foam-crested reefs of these largely uncharted seas were the most dangerous menace. Many a whale ship left her bones on the coral, and many a New England sailor died on the reefs or found uncertain shelter with the unpredictable South Sea islanders. In 1836 Horace Holden published a little book describing the adventures and sufferings of the survivors of the whaleship *Mentor,* Captain Edward Bonnard, which was wrecked on a reef of the Palau group in the western Carolines on May 21, 1832. Of the crew of twenty-two, half were lost. The surviving eleven men, including Captain Bonnard and Holden, a farm boy from Hillsborough, New Hampshire, who was on his first voyage, got away in the one remaining boat and reached a sandspit on the lee side of the lagoon. In the distance a small island could be seen, from which natives soon arrived who relieved them of guns, cutlasses, and clothing. A few days later the sailors reached Babelthuap Island, the largest of the Palau group, where they were adopted by one of the native tribes and where they found a tattooed Englishman who had lived there for thirty years. The natives helped build a large canoe. Upon its completion eight New Englanders with three natives set sail for the Celebes in the canoe and the whale boat. (The other three sailors had taken native wives and decided to remain on Babelthuap.) The second day out the canoe capsized and all eleven men, suffering from thirst, continued their voyage in the overloaded whale boat.

On December 6, 1832, they drifted near Tobi or Lord North Island about half way between the Palaus and Celebes, where they were captured and kept in slavery by the natives of that remote little land. They were the first white men to set foot on the island although it had been discovered in 1767.

On February 3, 1833, a ship appeared, but only Captain Bonnard and one sailor were able to get on board. The six

Yankees left on Tobi were all forcefully tattooed. Another ship, which appeared August 3, sailed off without being aware of the stranded men. In nineteen months on Tobi four of the white men and two of the Caroline Islanders died of starvation and mistreatment. On Thanksgiving Day, 1834, Horace Holden and his friend Benjamin Nute, the only two white survivors on Tobi, were rescued by the bark *Britannia,* Captain Henry Short, and taken to Canton from where, after several weeks' recuperation, they were returned to New York. Holden, with the help of the Reverend John Pickering of Boston, wrote *A Narrative of the Shipwreck, Captivity, and Suffering of Horace Holden and Benjamin Nute,* and by its sale raised enough money to take him to Washington to plead in Congress for the rescue of the men on Babelthuap. In the meantime, however, two of the men were rescued by the U.S.S. *Vincennes* and arrived in Hampton Roads, Virginia. The third man had already escaped on another ship.[16]

❋

There was one very pleasant aspect of whaling and the abundant evidence of it in collections along the New England seaboard is as attractive as it is ingenious. Whalers carried large crews for the size of the ships for they needed many more men to man the whale boats than a merchant vessel required. But these large crews meant that the men had endless hours at sea with time on their hands, time often devoted to scrimshawing— the art of carving in bone or wood or ivory. Some of the results of this time-consuming craft were useful—belaying pins, fids, clothespins, handles for tools, bootjacks, and what not. Swifts for winding yarn and jagging wheels to put the crimp in the edges of pies were made to bring home to the womenfolks.

NEW ENGLAND AND THE SOUTH SEAS

Other things were purely decorative, the favorites being ornamental whales' teeth and, less commonly, walrus' tusks. Teeth and tusks were engraved with freehand drawings of ships, whales, landfalls, or other pictures or designs that struck the artist's fancy. For more sophisticated products, woodcuts or engravings from Godey's *Lady's Book,* the *Naval Annual,* or other magazines were pasted on the teeth and etched through. The picture was then removed and the etching colored. Some of these engraved teeth are works of art, some are historical, some are humorous. Carved busks for corsets were popular in the days when stays were a fashionable necessity. They, too, were often inscribed with verses, one of which reads. "This bone once in a sperm whale's jaw did rest. Now 'tis intended for a woman's breast. This my love I do intend for you to wear and

not to lend." Other inscriptions on scrimshaw referred to the pursuit itself, such as, "Death to the living, long life to the killers, success to sailor's wives, and greasy luck to whalers." Broadly speaking, the engravings can be divided into patriotic subjects, ships and whaling scenes, and those of a sentimental variety.

Whale teeth were also valuable articles to barter with the natives for hogs, fruits, and vegetables—the fresh food so necessary to keep men healthy on a long cruise. Nothing was prized more highly in Tonga and the Fijis than a fine large whale tooth—which was worn as a chiefly

10. Scrimshawed whale's tooth

symbol. Not only did the whalers swap them directly with the Pacific Islanders, they also sold or exchanged them to traders going to the islands for sandalwood or bêche-de-mer, who found them equally good specie.

Whaling was a business in which risks were great, not, as one might suppose, from ship losses which seldom exceeded one percent of the fleet a year, or from labor troubles which were cushioned by the lay system, but by the fluctuation in prices and the demand for products. Because of the length of whaling voyages, prices at the inception of a voyage did not necessarily bear any relation to those at its termination. Losses were sometimes heavy but profits could be enormous. Protection against losses were provided by the lay system, multiple ownership of vessels by fractional shares, and marine insurance.

In his *Narrative of the United States Exploring Expedition,* Wilkes wrote: "Our whaling fleet may be said at this very day to whiten the Pacific Ocean with its canvas, and the proceeds of this fishery give comfort and happiness to many thousands of our citizens." [17] The whaling fleet at that time numbered 675 vessels grossing over 200,000 tons, the majority of which were cruising the Pacific. It took between 15,000 and 16,000 hands to man these vessels and the whaling industry on shore in New England employed at least twice as many men as were at sea. The value of this fleet was estimated at not less than twenty-five million dollars with the annual return yielding some five million dollars. Five principal products arrived on whalers coming from the Pacific. The sperm whale yielded sperm oil of high quality for lubrication and illumination, spermaceti for candles, and ambergris for the manufacture of perfumes and as an aphrodisiac in Moslem countries. The baleen whales produced whale oil, heavier and inferior to sperm but used for the same purposes, and whalebone whose tough flexible quality made it the ideal material for corset stays, umbrellas, whips, and other manufactures. About one quarter of the annual catch of sperm oil, whale oil, and whalebone was exported, much to Germany, the Low Countries, France, and England.

Whaling reached its peak in the 1840's and 1850's. With the Civil War began a series of calamitous events which, in combination with the depletion of whales and the discovery of other natural products, doomed the industry. The massive blows began with the sinking of the Great Stone Fleet. In November 1861 forty old whale ships, mostly from New Bedford and New London, purchased by the federal government, were loaded with stone and sunk to blockade Charleston and Savannah harbors. This tonnage was never replaced in the whaling fleet. The *Alabama* and other Confederate raiders wrecked havoc on the whaling fleet in the Atlantic, often lurking along the courses habitually sailed by Pacific whalers outward and homeward bound. In 1865 the Confederate cruiser *Shenandoah,* under Captain James I. Waddell, entered the Pacific and captured thirty-nine whalers, burning all but five. This virtually eliminated the Pacific–Arctic whaling fleet. Whaling received its most massive blow in 1871 when the fleet of ships which had gone into the Pacific and through the Bering Strait for Arctic whaling was caught in the ice near Point Belcher and had to be abandoned. Thirty-three vessels (twenty-two from New Bedford represented almost two million dollars in capital investment) were lost, and five escaping ships brought over a thousand seamen from Icy Cape to Honolulu. Five years later twelve more were lost in the ice, and in 1888

HUNTING THE CACHALOT

five more went down off Point Barrow, Alaska. For all intents and purposes American whaling in the Pacific was no more.

This series of disasters would not have killed an entire industry had not it already been doomed by other, less dramatic but more wasting, factors. Whales were becoming scarcer making voyages longer and more expensive. Petroleum products replaced oil for lubrication and illumination, relegating whale oil lamps and spermaceti candles to the attic. Only whalebone had no immediate substitute, and there were some late whaling voyages for bone alone.

For over seventy-five years whalemen had swarmed around the coasts and islands of the Pacific where their impact on native populations, influence upon the rise of towns and cities, and changes in the sea mammal population is still apparent. The influence of the Pacific whaling resources on New England is still apparent also, for the wealth they brought provided a substantial part of the money to finance the rise of the textile mills and speed up the region's industrial revolution.

III ~

SEA OTTERS AND SANDALWOOD

John Ledyard's exuberant attempts to interest his fellow Americans in voyages to the Northwest Coast for sea otter skins had fallen on deaf ears. In 1784, however, the official published account of Cook's voyages appeared, and the rumors which Ledyard and others on the expedition had been circulating were verified; Cook himself recommended the sea otter trade as a lucrative enterprise. The Russians were already trading a few sea otter pelts each year through Kyakhta on the Chinese–Siberian border, where all their trade with China was conducted. Following Bering's expedition, they had pushed eastward from their Siberian bases along the Aleutian chain.

What was this animal whose fur was so much more valuable than the finest Siberian fox or sable or marten skin to the Chinese? The sea otter, which superficially has some resemblance to the seal, is an entirely different animal, unique among marine mammals. There are two races of this singular creature. The northern race ranges from the northernmost islands of Japan past the Kuril group and Kamchatka to the Aleutians and down the northwest coast of America. The southern race is found off the coast of California and Lower California. The fur is of exceptional beauty, being unusually fine, soft, and thick. At the base it is a shining white or silver which darkens to the ends in various shades of brown which are lustrous, brightened with silvery overhairs. The darkest brown, known as black in the trade, are the choice pelts. According to John Jewitt, the tail fur is finer and closer set than elsewhere on the animal and brought a premium in the China market.[1] For this reason the Indians cut off the tail and sold it separately. In general, size was the determining factor in a skin value and a prime skin reached from a man's chin to the ground. The remark of William Sturgis, a veteran Nor'west man from Boston, that the sea otter was exceeded in loveliness only by a beautiful woman or a comely infant, has been quoted many times.[2]

These creatures, until disturbed by hunters, led a peaceful and rather idyllic existence. Their lives seem to have been spent in complete tranquillity, floating contentedly upon their backs with their forepaws on their breasts. They lay thus, side by side, in groups of about a hundred, riding up and down with the ocean swells on the buoyant kelp beds. Occasionally they dove for food and, bringing up a shellfish, used their forepaws as hands, still lying on their backs, to eat in a leisurely, polite manner. Their hind legs were quite different from the short, thick forelimbs, being longer, with webbed feet and a more flipperlike appearance. The tail, which served mostly as a rudder, was less than a foot long by about two and a half inches wide, and rather stiff. On land these beasts, five feet long and weighing eighty pounds, proceeded awkwardly but rapidly in a series of quick jumps.

Once disturbed by hunters, the sea otter presented an entirely different appearance. The herds dispersed for greater safety, and the animals could project themselves through the water with remarkable speed, resorting to intricate maneuvers to throw the pursuer off the track, sometimes making several quick dives and then a long one, reversing direction and attempting to get in among the breakers and rocks away from the boats.

The Nor'westers depended entirely on native hunters for skins. The most skillful of these were the Aleuts who silently paddled their skin-covered kayaks or bidarkas into a herd and dispatched the animals with light arrow-headed harpoons cast with the added impetus of a throwing stick. Some of the Indian tribes set nets for otters in the kelp beds or killed them with clubs when they sought shelter from a storm along rocky shores.

The Chinese market was far from satisfied in its demand for the beautiful sea otter skins. Besides the trickle coming in by way of Siberia from the Russians, skins from California began to arrive in China on the Manila galleons. Between seven and eight hundred were shipped on the *Princesa* from Acapulco in 1783, but the number was still small. In China the price kept going up, until by 1790 a prime skin brought from eighty to one hundred and twenty dollars in the Chinese market. Mandarins sported sea otter robes and women of wealth wore capes made from the fur. The fur also served as background for pearls on belts and sashes, for caps, mittens, and trimmings of clothing, and, especially, as the price became more prohibitive, as borders for rich silk gowns. It was into this market that Cook's sailors brought their few otter skins and made a profit which seemed unbelievable. No wonder Ledyard was frantic trying to find someone to finance an expedition for him!

SEA OTTERS AND SANDALWOOD

The Northwest Coast fur trade was begun by the English, but, because of the monopolies of the South Sea Company and the East India Company, it was a difficult business for them. The South Sea Company owned the monopoly for trade on the western coast of America, and the East India Company had license on the Asiatic side. The result was that the British trader could obtain his product only within the limits of one company and it was only salable within the monopoly of the other. It was very difficult to obtain licenses from the two companies and then only on the strictest terms, with the result that this lucrative Pacific Ocean trade was for all practical purposes closed to them unless they operated under foreign colors, as some of them did.

But Americans were not slow to enter the field. Soon it became a trade associated especially with Boston, for it was carried on largely by Boston merchants for over forty years. It began when Joseph Barrell of Boston completed reading of Cook's third voyage and decided that a commodity so eagerly sought after in China should be taken to the Chinese. He organized a group of adventurers: Joseph Barrell, Charles Bulfinch, Samuel Brown, Crowell Hatch, and Marden Pintard from Boston and John Derby of Salem. These six men purchased two vessels and outfitted them at a cost of fifty thousand dollars. The ship *Columbia Rediviva,* commonly known in history as the *Columbia,* was of 212 tons, built in 1787 at Plymouth. The *Lady Washington,* commonly known as the *Washington,* a sloop of 90 tons, was to act as a tender for the *Columbia* in accordance with a plan outlined in Captain Cook's account. The two vessels sailed for the Northwest Coast the last day of September 1787, under the command of Captain John Kendrick of Wareham, Massachusetts, master of the *Columbia,* and Captain Robert Gray of Tiverton, Rhode Island, in the

11. Ship *Columbia* in winter quarters on the Northwest Coast

Washington. After being separated in a gale off of Cape Horn, both arrived at a rendezvous in Nootka Sound, Vancouver Island, in September where they remained until the following March. Gray in the sloop ranged the coast, trading with the Indians, from Juan de Fuca Strait north to Bucareli Bay, Alaska. He did very well. In the Queen Charlotte Islands in a very few moments he secured two hundred sea otter skins at the rate of one chisel each. The skins collected by the sloop were transferred to the ship and, for some unknown reason, the two captains exchanged commands. Gray, taking over the *Columbia,* sailed for China by way of the Hawaiian Islands and returned to Boston, August 9, 1790, the first American vessel to circumnavigate the globe. Captain Kendrick continued to trade on the coast until January 1790, when he arrived in China with a cargo of sea otter skins which he sold for $18,000.

SEA OTTERS AND SANDALWOOD

This first voyage was not a financial success, due principally to Kendrick's appropriation of the *Washington* and her cargo, and also to damage in the *Columbia's* cargo of teas, but it did well enough so that it was decided to send Captain Gray again in the *Columbia*. She was fitted for the second voyage in the remarkably short time of six weeks, and sailed on September 28, 1790, reaching the coast in early June of the following year. A sloop named the *Adventure,* which had been brought out on board in frames, was set up and sent along the coast trading for furs. On this voyage Captain Gray established his country's claims to the Oregon territory when he sailed the *Columbia* over the bar into the great river named for his ship. Laden with sea otter skins, Gray sold the *Adventure* to the Spaniards and went on to China where he disposed of his cargo, loaded the *Columbia* with Oriental goods, and continued homeward, arriving in Boston on July 29, 1793. Seldom has a trader achieved fame for himself and his ship on two successive voyages, but Captain Robert Gray and the *Columbia* accomplished that feat. His course was rarely deviated from by later captains. Following Captain Gray's voyage the Hawaiian Islands became the regular stopping place for all vessels carrying furs from the Northwest Coast to China.

❄

The maritime fur trade of the Northwest Coast lasted forty years, from 1785 to 1825, and for the first three years of that period it was entirely English. Gray and Kendrick were the pioneers of American ascendency. For Yankees, sea otters, like the ginseng or anything else salable in the China market, were nothing more than desirable mediums of exchange for obtaining teas, silks, nankeens, porcelains, and other Oriental goods

12. Ships *Midas* and *Levant* off Lintin Island, China

for sale in the United States or for export, from which they made their cash profit. The English, for the reasons already mentioned, could not compete as, while they might obtain licenses to transport furs to the Canton market, once there, because of the East India Company monopoly, they could not trade independently. The Company was adamant on this point and the best a fur trader could hope for was to carry a cargo for the East India Company to England. Since the great profit was on the China products end, the English flag virtually disappeared from the Northwest Coast by 1801.

During the early period of the trade, skins were obtained by bartering directly with the natives. Nails, beads, mirrors, buttons, and other trinkets first served the purpose, but soon the Indians were demanding chisels, hatchets, knives, bar iron, sheet copper, firearms, blankets, cooking dishes, and similar useful things. It was sometimes cheaper to buy trade goods in Europe than in America. For instance, Captain John Salter in the ship *Boston* of Boston, took on a cargo of trade goods in Hull, England, for the Northwest Coast. This cargo included English cloth and Dutch blankets as well as looking glasses, beads, knives, and razors imported from Holland. Sugar, molasses, and twenty hogsheads of rum were put aboard and, probably most valuable of all, three thousand muskets and fowling pieces along with a large quantity of ammunition, cutlasses, and pistols. Captain Salter also took on board as armorer, John R. Jewitt, one of the only two survivors of the calamitous Indian capture of the *Boston* at Nootka Sound who later wrote an adventurous account of his captivity. Most of Jewitt's time on the outward passage was spent, "putting in order some of the muskets, and making daggers, knives, and some small hatchets for the Indian trade." And again he remarks that his time was constantly occupied "in re-fitting or repairing some of the iron work of the vessel, but principally in making tomahawks, daggers, etc. for the North West Coast." [3]

In 1803 Captain Joseph O'Cain in the ship *O'Cain,* trading for the Winships of Boston, made an efficient and productive contract with the Russian Governor of Alaska, Alexander Baranov. In return for one half the skins, Baranov guaranteed to supply Aleut hunters with their bidarkas who would live on and hunt from the *O'Cain* as she searched out sea otter herds. Since the Russians lacked ships and the Yankees could not hunt for themselves, this worked out for the mutual benefit of both parties and became the prevailing system for the next nine years, until the War of 1812 made it too uncertain from a Russian viewpoint.

Ships from Boston, on their way to the Northwest Coast

via Cape Horn, found that by a few weeks' delay at Juan Fernández, and especially Más Afuera off the Chilean coast, a dozen or fifteen thousand fur sealskins could be collected. These could be sold for about five dollars apiece in Canton ten times their value in the New York market. As long as the seals held out, the sealskin market continued to be profitable, with prices fluctuating between the high and as low as thirty-five cents each. Seals also abounded on the coasts of Chile and Peru and of Baja California. Americans were forbidden to hunt here by the Spanish, but that did not prevent them, and organized poaching developed upon a scale far beyond anything before known. This illegal hunting combined with smuggling on the indifferently patrolled and protected Spanish coast became the largest and one of the most profitable of all the illicit trades, and added to the diversification of the cargoes going to China. With sealskins, sea otters, land animals, sandalwood, and other products from the islands, the trading ships became more roving in their movements.

The sealers wrote more than the Nor'westmen, and accounts of their activities and adventures in the interesting books of captains Edmund Fanning and Benjamin Morrell of Stonington, Connecticut, and Amasa Delano of Duxbury, Massachusetts, give a detailed picture of the business.[4]

Captain Fanning in the brig *Betsey* of New York City is typical of the early period. He was in the Pacific by January 1798, having stopped at Patagonia and the Falkland Islands on the way. On January 20 he was at Más Afuera where he lost one boat in the surf and nearly lost some of his men who were forced to spend several cold, wet nights ashore before another boat could get in to them. The sealing was very successful. While the sealers were washing out the sealskins at the water's edge and tossing scraps of meat and blubber into the water, sea bass and other fish arrived in such ravenous multitudes that the men killed the fish by hitting them on their heads with seal clubs. By April 2 a full cargo of skins was obtained. In fact, so many did they have and so anxious were they to be sure of filling the ship, that after the hold was stowed they then filled much of the cabin and finally the forecastle, leaving just enough space for accommodation of the ship's company. They still had four thousand sealskins in stacks left over and the boatswain and boat's crew were left to take charge of them and add to the stock until another vessel from their owners should call. Once the skins were stowed for a few days they settled, and after a couple of weeks the forecastle and cabin could be cleared. In ten weeks they had a full cargo for the Canton market, and Fanning estimated that when he left Más Afuera there were between five and seven hundred thousand fur seals on it. Shortly afterward about a million were taken from the island and nearly all carried to Canton to exchange for China goods. The *Betsey* left Más Afuera April 5 and on May 20 hove to abreast a verdant valley covered with breadfruit and coconut trees at Hiva Oa in the Marquesas Islands. It was the captain's intention to trade with the natives, refresh his crew, and take on fresh provisions. These stops at Pacific Islands had a very salubrious effect upon the ship's company. Fanning says, "The fragrance of these green valleys brought off to us by flows of wind at intervals was truly delicious and a person who has at no time enjoyed it can scarcely be able to conceive with what delight we received it, after having been for a length of time at sea. It actually seems to take hold upon the feelings in such a manner as to reanimate the whole system." [5]

Fanning was unable to get any provisions although he was offered four human skulls which decorated the bow of one of the large canoes. He was about to penetrate farther into a bay when, on May 22, he saw a small canoe approaching with two men in it. They were both dressed in native style, but one of them turned out to be the Reverend William Pascoe Crook who had come out to the Marquesas from the London Mis-

13. Resolution Bay, Marquesas Islands

sionary Society with Captain Henry Wilson on the missionary ship *Duff*. The man with him was a friendly chief, but Crook informed Fanning that a renegade Italian sailor with a musket and ammunition had established his authority among the local natives, was promoting wars between the tribes, and wished to entice Fanning's ship close in shore where it was planned to pull her aground and overwhelm the crew. Crook's own life was in danger and the captain agreed to take him back to the United States if he wished. Fanning lost no time in getting out of the dangerous situation and sailing to the northern Marquesas. They were received in a friendly manner at Nuku Hiva and were able to fill their water casks for a voyage to Canton. Mr. Crook who had learned the native language was invaluable as an interpreter, and such amiable relations were established that he decided to stay on Nuku Hiva. Besides water, Fanning took on a number of large fat hogs and some smaller pigs, fowls, yams, and breadfruit—all welcome fresh provisions. Amicable relations were nearly destroyed when one of the natives who was visiting on shipboard jumped out the cabin window with the azimuth compass. After an explanation to the chiefs of the importance of the compass to the ship and a demonstration of the ship's firearms, two chiefs came back with the stolen compass lacking the vane. The compass was repaired, the missing vane returned the next morning, and friendly relations were resumed. The chiefs offered to knock the thief on the head with a club, but Fanning, having no wish to see him punished so severely, simply requested them to keep the man away from the ship. At the time of Fanning's visit to the Marquesas, hogs, fowls, breadfruit, coconuts, yams, and taro were plentiful, and he remarked that their sugar cane was the finest and largest that he had ever seen. He considered the rates for supplies reasonable; a pig weighing forty to sixty pounds was purchased with a small fishhook, board nail, or bit of iron hoop three of four inches long. The sealers also bought many fathoms of native fishing lines and ropes made of a tree bark which they found could be used for replacing running rigging.

Captain Fanning set up rules for dealing and trading with the natives. Any crew member who broke them was confined in the ship's run until such time as she should leave the islands. One officer was appointed to superintend trading, inspecting all purchases received on board as well as any article exchanged or sold to the natives. This arrangement apparently worked well and there was only one rather innocent infraction of the rules while he was there.

Leaving the Reverend Crook and his Marquesan friends on May 30, 1798, the *Betsey* set sail for China where Fanning traded his sealskins for China goods and continued on around the world. He dropped anchor off his home town of Stonington on April 18, 1799, then he continued through Long Island Sound and arrived at New York on the 26th, after a passage of one hundred and seventy-eight days from Canton. After the deduction of all charges, including cost of the ship and outfits, his owners divided a net profit of $52,300. Fanning remarks that the duties paid into the National Treasury on the voyage amounted to more than three times the cost of the ship and her gear.

Captain Fanning's fellow townsman, Benjamin Morrell, Jr., was engaged in the same adventurous trade between 1822 and 1831. Running away from home as a boy to go to sea, he had been captured twice by the British in the War of 1812 and held prisoner both at St. John's, Newfoundland, and in Dartmoor Prison, England. On July 1, 1822 Morrell set out with the schooner *Wasp* from New York for fur seals and sea elephants. He evidently believed in the good life, for three days later, on the Fourth of July, he fired a salute and related: "The crew on this occasion were furnished with an extra allowance of such good things as tended to enliven their patriotism and brighten their ideas of national glory, during the discussion of which we of the quarter-deck were not niggardly in setting them a good example."[6] After going the usual way to the Falklands, the islands around Cape Horn, Juan Fernández, and the Galapagos, he had trouble with the Spanish authorities on the coast of Chile. He ended up by selling his vessel and bringing his cargo of sealskins back to the United States on board the Salem ship *Endeavor* owned by Silsbee, Pickman and Stone, under Captain Elwell. On his second voyage, after hunting along the California coast, he was at the Sandwich Islands for the usual refreshment, but then returned to the west coast, the Galapagos, and back to New York with his skins instead of going on to China. Morrell's fourth trading voyage in a little 172-ton schooner called the *Antarctic* covered a great deal of the Pacific. He took his departure from Sandy Hook, Connecticut, on September 2, 1829, and did not return to his home port until nearly two years later on August 27, 1831. In the course of that voyage he made extended stays at the Bay of Islands in New Zealand, in the Fijis, and at Manila.

Captain Amasa Delano, one of the most enterprising and unscrupulous sealers and Pacific traders, was born in Duxbury, Massachusetts, February 21, 1763, and named for an unfortunate uncle who was killed by the Indians while an officer in Rogers' Rangers.* Amasa cared little for schooling and went to sea at an early age. After serving an apprenticeship in coasting, transatlantic voyages, and the West Indies trade, he cruised around the Pacific in the ship *Perserverance,* collecting sealskins, trading for sandalwood, picking up cargoes of China goods, and turning a penny wherever he could. In 1800 he was sealing at Más Afeura. He remarks that when the Americans came there about 1797 there were between two and three million seals on the island, and that he himself had

---

* Rogers' Rangers were the famous group of raiders from New England led by Robert Rogers during the French and Indian War.

NEW ENGLAND AND THE SOUTH SEAS

taken more than a hundred thousand skins there. In 1809 he was off Easter Island where a landing attempt was prevented by heavy surf.

Later the same year Delano was at the Galapagos Islands collecting land tortoises which, he claimed, could be trained like domestic animals. "The method to effect this is, by whipping them with a small line when they are out of place, and to take them up and carry them to the place assigned for them, which being repeated a few times will bring them into the practice of going themselves, by being whipped when they are out of their place. They can be taught to eat on board a ship as well as a sheep, or a goat, and will live for a long time if there is proper food provided for them." He further comments, "I carried at one time from James's Island three hundred very good terrapins to the island of Massa Fuero; and there landed more than one half of them, after having them sixty days on board my ship. Half of the number landed, died as soon as they took food. This was owing to their stomachs having got so weak and out of tone, that they could not digest it. As soon as they eat any grass after landing, they would froth at the mouth, and appeared to be in a state of insanity, and died in the course of a day or two." [7] It was customary for traders and whalers to carry off the large land tortoises. The flesh was favored by sailors for duff and the water in their bladders was fresh and sweet.

Later in 1801 Delano was at the Hawaiian Islands taking on sandalwood. He also took five Hawaiians (two purposely; the other three were stowaways) and carried them to Canton. He brought one, a boy whom he named Bill, to Boston, where he "performed on the Boston stage several times in the Tragedy of Captain Cook, and was much admired by the audience and the public in general." [8] (Delano later returned Bill to Hawaii,

SEA OTTERS AND SANDALWOOD

but the islander did not wish to remain there and went on to Canton where he disappeared.)

The Hawaiian Islanders raised dogs as well as pigs for meat, but only the latter could be sold to New Englanders as ship's supplies. Occasionally venturesome Yankees tried exotic foods, sometimes unwittingly. In the Hawaiian Islands Delano was accustomed to sup with a group of congenial captains.

It happened one day while we were at dinner, that the conversation turned upon having a dog cooked and served up with the rest of our good fare. One of the company observed that we had not had one. I made reply, that I did not desire to have one cooked for our table, as I had a peculiar prejudice against eating these animals . . . I was answered, that I should not know the difference between a dog and a pig when it was cooked. The next day at dinner two pigs, as they called them, were brought on to the table; one was without a head, which was placed opposite to where I sat. I was very politely asked what I would be helped to? My answer was, a piece of pig. The gentleman who sat near the one which had no head, asked if he should help me to a piece of it, which was baked in that country stile; and said that he would recommend it far before the other, which was roasted. Yes, was my answer. I was helped and eat very heartily of it. The gentleman who had helped me, said, that there was a plenty more that I could be helped to if I like it. My reply was that I never tasted any thing better, and was again helped, and finished my dinner or what I thought to be the baked pig.

In the course of the afternoon there were many jokes passed on the subject of eating dogs, till at last I began to suspect that some trick had been played upon me. After inquiring into the affair, they satisfied me that what I had made so hearty a meal of was a dog. It caused some disagreeable sensation for the moment, and I was a little angry; but on reflection, and seeing my comrades make themselves merry at my expense, I thought it was the most prudent way to turn it off with a laugh. I sincerely believe that eating of the dog has not done me any harm, unless it was, that I possibly might have partook a little more largely of the canine spirit.[9]

Amasa Delano is probably representative of the New England captains who were in the Pacific in the early nineteeth century; yet, what manner of man could write the following after his boat capsized off the Tasmanian coast!

> While moving my legs in the water endeavouring to keep myself up, I hit them against a bundle of small sticks that had been cut for the purpose of stringing the fish on; I got hold of it, and placed it under my breast; although it did not swim buoyant, it prevented me from sinking suddenly between the waves. I was just heading for the land, when looking to the left, I saw one of my faithful sailors, a Swede, by the name of John Fostram, making towards me with all possible exertion. I turned my head from him, and used every effort to prevent his reaching me, which I greatly apprehended he would; but the poor fellow finding his attempts fail, relinquished the oar he had grasped in his hand, his head gradually lowering, until his strength being entirely exhausted, he gave up, and sunk. I never until then had experienced any satisfaction at seeing a man die; but so great is the regard we have for ourselves when in danger, that we would sooner see the whole human race perish than die ourselves. I remember but few incidents in the course of my life, that were more gratifying to me than that of Fostram's sinking; for I was not only relieved of the dread of his involving me in his own fate, but had likewise the oar he relinquished within my reach, which I immediately seized, and headed again for the land. Very soon after I observed another of my poor distressed sailors, a native of Nova Scotia, named William Thompson, making towards me on the right hand. I pulled from him, though he did not give me so much uneasiness as the former, as he was at a greater distance. This poor fellow soon met his fate in a similar manner with Fostram. I likewise made shift to procure his oar, and placed it under me, and then once more headed for the land.[10]

Some of the sealers not only took skins to the China market but also brought them back to the United States or Europe. Skins obtained in the South Atlantic, South Pacific, or the Antarctic were prepared differently for the two markets. Those going to China were stretched and dried; those intended for the American or European markets, while wet, were salted and booked or kentched.

Both Northwesters and sealers stopped at the Hawaiian Islands. As sea otters became scarce, ships from the Northwest Coast, when they could not obtain a cargo of otter skins in one season, often wintered in the Islands, returning the following spring to complete their cargo. It was not long before some astute mariner discovered that the Hawaiian Islands themselves produced a very desirable commodity for the China market. Sandalwood used as incense and for small boxes brought high prices in China, where it was intensely desired, and the demand was greater than the quantity of wood from India then available. By the early nineteenth century trade in the aromatic wood was a standard part of the Northwest Coast—Hawaiian Islands course which began in Boston and ended in China.

Captain Robert Gray's colleague, John Kendrick (who never returned to Boston, but continued in the *Lady Washington* plying between the Northwest Coast and China until he was accidentally killed during the firing of a salute in the Hawaiian Islands in 1793), left three men in the islands in 1789 and three more in 1791 to collect sandalwood and pearls. He is generally credited with taking the first Hawaiian wood to Canton, but this is by no means certain. His friend Captain William Douglas had also left two men on Kauai to gather sandalwood in 1790, and that same year Captain Amasa Delano said that he had seen more than twenty tons of Hawaiian wood at Canton.

After these early attempts to introduce Hawaiian sandalwood into the Canton market, there is little mention of it in actual trading until more than twenty years later when the Winship brothers and Captain William Heath Davis of Boston obtained from King Kamehameha I a ten-year monopoly of sandalwood and cotton produced in the Islands. Captains Jonathan and Nathan Winship were already successful veterans of the Northwest Coast fur trade when they sailed from Boston in 1809 in command of the ships *Albatross* and *O'Cain*.

In 1811 they met Captain Davis in the *Isabella* at Honolulu and, after completing their cargo with sandalwood, sailed for Canton. The profit on the wood was sufficient to bring the three men back to Honolulu three months later. The monopoly with the king was successfully negotiated, and the Winships

14. King Kamehameha I

withdrew from the fur trade and settled down to enjoy the sandalwood business safe from competition. Kamehameha was to receive one-quarter of the value of the wood and cotton taken from the Islands by Winship, Winship, and Davis. The arrangement, unfortunately for the Winships, was short-lived, for in 1813, when Kamehameha heard of the War of 1812, he repudiated the contract.

SEA OTTERS AND SANDALWOOD

A few examples of Northwest Coast and Hawaiian Islands voyages will show the usual procedure. In 1791 Captain J. Prince took Samuel Shaw's 800-ton ship *Massachusetts,* fitted out like an English East Indiaman, to China. The *Massachusetts* was the largest and handsomest American ship to enter the China trade, but she arrived with a damaged cargo and her condition was such that the owners took a great loss and prejudiced Boston merchants against using vessels of more than half her size for years thereafter. She was, therefore, sold to the Dutch in China. John Bartlett, one of the seamen, shipped on the brig *Gustavus* for a voyage to the Northwest Coast where he arrived in early March 1791. They arrived on the coast suffering from scurvy and a couple of the sailors died before enough greens could be obtained to offset the disease. Cruising up and down the coast, they picked up 70 sea otter skins here, 200 there, and 400 at another place, until by June 10, when they bought 19 skins, the total was 1218. By July 4 the number of skins had risen to 1683, and on July 16, they sailed with 1869 skins. On August 23 they arrived at Hawaii and came abreast Kealakekua Bay, arriving only a short time after a tragic incident which caused a great deal of hard feeling between the whites and the Hawaiians.

In late 1789 Captain Simon Metcalf of New York in the brig *Eleanora* stopped at the Islands with his cargo of furs. His eighteen-year-old son was in command of the schooner *Fair American.* While the *Eleanora* was lying off Maui the chief of Olowalu and some of his men stole one of the vessel's boats from its moorings at the stern, murdering a sailor who was sleeping in it. They broke the boat up to get the nails. Captain Metcalf found out where the men had come from, and took the *Eleanora* over to Olowalu. He ordered his guns loaded with grapeshot, got his vessel ready for action, and had one of the chiefs taboo one side of the ship so that all of the natives would swarm around the other side. Metcalf had beads thrown overboard to attract as many as possible and about three hundred canoes assembled. He then fired his broadside, killing over a hundred men, women, and children and wounding many more. Some two weeks later the *Fair American* was approached by a fleet of trading canoes, and the younger Metcalf was caught off guard. The Hawaiians threw him overboard, killed all of the crew except the mate Isaac Davis, and hauling the vessel on shore, stripped her of guns and ammunition. The same or the next day John Young, boatswain of the *Eleanora,* who was on shore, was detained by the orders of Kamehameha himself in order to keep Captain Metcalf from hearing of the death of his son and the loss of the *Fair American.* The *Eleanora* sailed off to China without Young, and Captain Metcalf knew nothing of his son's death. Young and Davis, both Englishmen, remained in the Islands and became the principal advisors to King Kamehameha.

The redoubtable Salem voyager Captain Richard Cleveland made a remarkable trip in 1799 from China to the Northwest Coast in an attempt to recoup his fortunes. He bought a small cutter and sailed her into the teeth of the monsoon season in order to arrive early on the Coast and get back to China with his cargo before the shipments arrived and depressed the price of skins. Sailing from Canton on January 10, he worked his way through the China Sea, keeping close to the coast to duck in out of each storm. Headwinds and heavy weather made it slow going. Part of the crew mutinied and had to be left ashore. After an extraordinary crossing of the northern Pacific he arrived at Norfolk Sound, British Columbia, on March 30, and immediately engaged in a busy traffic with the Indians. Only one or two ships had beaten him there and he secured a great number of skins singly or in small lots. The small size of his vessel was helpful for he could cruise in restricted waters where larger ships could not penetrate. After collecting about two thousand skins he returned to China by way of the Sandwich Islands to the amazement of his friends in Canton who could scarcely believe that he had already been to the coast and returned with a cargo valued at about $60,000.

In 1802, Captain Cleveland was again on the coast as mate of the *Lelia Byrd* under Captain William Shaller. After various adventures on the South American and California coasts, where they purchased some horses to take to the Sandwich Islands, they arrived at Kealakekua Bay, June 21. The horses were the first ever imported to the Islands and caused an enormous amount of curiosity and excitement. Multitudes of natives came to see them and their amazement reached its climax when one of the sailors mounted a horse and galloped up and down the beach. Only the king refused to show any sign of surprise or wonder, but he did remark that the horses would be a sufficient compensation for the food which the ship required. The *Lelia Byrd* arrived at Canton on August 29, 1803. Captain Cleveland left her there and returned to Boston on the ship *Alert*.

With the exception of the uncertain Kendrick and Douglas enterprises, no mention is made of sandalwood on these early voyages which called at the Hawaiian Islands. John Kendrick had made two attempts to institute a trade in it, by leaving men there to collect sandalwood while he was on the coast and have it ready for him to pick up on his return. His plans never materialized, but a decade later this had become an additional reason for stopping at the Islands en route to China. By 1810 various changes were being made in the fur trade. Sea otters were getting scarcer and their price on the Northwest Coast was going up. Ships in the trade, while they still wanted otter skins if they could get them, also took beaver, mink, and the furs of other land animals; and sealskins picked up off South America helped out. Conversely, the price of sea otters in China was going down, for the great quantity brought into Canton in a few years' time had glutted the market. With profits reduced on both ends, the margin was decidedly smaller than in the early days. A good example of the changing trade is provided by the 1810–1813 voyage of the Salem brig *New Hazard*. She shopped around the Northwest Coast for furs and dickered for sandalwood in the Hawaiian Islands before obtaining sufficient cargo to continue on to China. It was on this voyage that eighteen-year-old Stephen Reynolds, of Boxford, Massachusetts, one of her sailors, got his first glimpse of Hawaii. Returning ten years later, he remained there for twenty-three years, ran a trading business, and became Master of the Port of Honolulu and an influential man in the Islands.

15. Stephen Reynolds, 1782–1857

The sandalwood trade was at its height between 1810 and 1825 and was sold in piculs of 133½ pounds each, with the price usually varying from eight to ten dollars per picul. This wood was the principal source of wealth of the Hawaiian kings and chiefs and with it they were able to buy guns and ammunition, liquor, schooners, Chinese silks, and other import goods for which they paid exorbitant prices. By 1825 sandalwood was no

SEA OTTERS AND SANDALWOOD

longer obtainable in the Hawaiian Islands. The avariciousness of both traders and chiefs had cleaned it out and glutted the Chinese market where the price dropped. It had gone the way of the sea otter.

Captain Edmund Fanning of Stonington, left a good account of the sandalwood business. Originally procured in India, the Americans found they could get it more cheaply in Hawaii, Fiji, and other mountainous islands of the Pacific where it was considered to be the property of the king or chief. Cut into four-foot lengths, the wood was so valuable that the slenderest limbs and twigs were taken, and it paid to dig the stump and roots out of the ground for they were only about 20 percent less valuable than the tree itself. The bark and sapwood were shaved off and every marketable scrap was saved. There were two kinds of sandalwood, so nearly identical in appearance that only an expert could differentiate between them. The spurious kind was to be avoided for it lost its fragrance in a short time. Many a man was chagrined, after taking wood to Canton, to discover that it was worthless and had to be thrown into the river to avoid paying a duty. Trees of medium age were the most desirable for the wood in old trees was often defective and worm-eaten and young trees were not as fragrant.

The Chinese merchants sorted sandalwood into four grades with a price range of from 20 to 70 percent between them. Luxury-loving, wealthy people in China had furniture manufactured from the sweet-smelling wood which filled the rooms with its odor. Fans, boxes, and other small articles were also made from it, but its commonest use was for joss sticks. The oil extracted from the wood was used for preparing small square sheets of gilt-edged joss paper. The paper, put up in packs and kept by the heads of families, was folded up, set on fire, and waved about whenever sickness or misfortune visited a member of the household.

When King Kamehameha I of the Hawaiian Islands died in 1819 he was succeeded by Liholiho who took the name of Kamehameha II. Under his reign the traders and whalers flourished in the Hawaiian Islands. He was, as S. E. Morison says, "A weak-minded and dissolute prince, [who] cheerfully stripped his royal domain in order to gratify tastes which the Boston traders stimulated. They sold him on credit rum and brandy, gin and champagne, carriages and harnesses, clothes and furniture, boats and vessels until he had tonnage and liquor enough for an old-time yacht club cruise." [11]

Boston traders competed to see how much sandalwood one could get out of Liholiho, and he worked his disgruntled subjects overtime to collect it in the mountains and satisfy his luxurious tastes. One of the things dangled in front of him successfully was the yacht *Cleopatra's Barge* sent out by the Boston firm of Bryant and Sturgis.

Cleopatra's Barge was the first ocean-cruising yacht built in America. The darling of George Crowninshield, Jr., of Salem, built by Retire Becket in 1816, was lavishly furnished in imitation of the royal yachts of Europe. Crowninshield made a well publicized cruise of the Mediterranean, but later died on board of a heart attack. After a few years in the merchant service, Bryant and Sturgis picked her up cheap to sell to the King of the Hawaiian Islands, and sent her out there under Captain John Suter with a cargo of axes, brandy, cottons, gin, hats, hardware, lead, looking glasses, molasses, muskets, swords, rum, dry goods, sugar, tea, wine, and books.

Suter arrived in Lahaina Roads, November 6, 1820, and within twenty-four hours the king and his retinue were on board. The king made two more visits to the vessel five and six days later, and Captain Suter gave him a five-gun salute. Ten days after Suter's arrival, Liholiho bought the *Barge* on credit for six thousand piculs of sandalwood to be made in future

SEA OTTERS AND SANDALWOOD

16. *Cleopatra's Barge*

deliveries. The agent for one of Bryant and Sturgis's competitors said she was the most enticing thing that had been shown to the king and that if Suter had held off a little longer he could have doubled his price.

Delighted with his new toy, Liholiho renamed her *Pride of Hawaii,* although to Americans she was still known as *Cleopatra's Barge.* The Reverend Hiram Bingham, who arrived in Hawaii in 1819, the year that the old king died, recorded morosely but faithfully how the king used his new toy.

> The King, having purchased on credit, the celebrated *Cleopatra's Barge,* built at Salem, Mass., and sold at the islands by Captain Suter, hastily

embarked on board her at Lahaina, and sailed for Honolulu, about the 3rd of February, 1821. Unexpectedly arriving at Honolulu, the firing of the guns at night in Waikiki Bay, announced the king's approach, and our village was soon in an uproar. The loud roar of the cannon from the *Cleopatra's Barge,* from the fort, and Punchbowl Hill—the successive flashing of their blaze on the dark curtain of the night, and the reverberating echoes from the hills and valleys of their report—the shouting of the noisy natives, and the voice of the crier demanding hogs, dogs, poi, etc., to be gathered for the reception of his majesty (who was in his cups), formed a combination of the sublime and the ridiculous not soon to be forgotten by the missionaries. The king landed Sabbath morning, amid the continuing noise, which was now increased by the yelping and crying dogs, tied on poles, and brought in for slaughter.[12]

And Walter Whitehill writes in his article on *Cleopatra's Barge,*

In July, when Liholiho, in a moment of drunken enthusiasm sailed the hundred miles to Kauai in an open boat, his five wives presently followed in *Cleopatra's Barge.* After several weeks spent in touring Kauai, Liholiho rewarded the hospitality of Kaumualii, king of the place, by kidnapping him and whisking him away to exile in Honolulu aboard the *Barge.* These nefarious and tipsy royal progresses, punctuated by salutes from forts and the barking of dogs, were interrupted in an edifying manner late in May 1823 when the king kindly offered free passage from Honolulu in his yacht to a group of missionaries bound to Lahaina. Bingham recorded with satisfaction how "the king and other members of the royal family, and several of the missionaries, assembling with this detachment on the quarterdeck of the brig, united in a parting hymn and prayer." Such godly interludes were, however, the exception rather than the rule.[13]

In 1823 Liholiho left the islands aboard a British whaler to visit his royal colleague George IV and to pay a visit to the President of the United States. While he was in England his yacht was driven ashore April 5, 1824 on the windward side of Kauai and completely wrecked. It was said that every person aboard the *Barge* at the time, except the captain, was intoxicated. The natives made a heroic effort to haul her off with great ropes of hibiscus bark twisted into cables which they fastened to the mainmast, but this was in vain. The mast broke off and the hull rolled into deeper water.

As both the northern sea otters and the sandalwood became scarcer, the products to be collected for the China trade became more diversified. Ships no longer could spend a pleasant summer on the Northwest Coast, retire to the Hawaiian Islands for the winter, and then return to the Northwest Coast to complete their cargo. They were forced to work the year round. They found that besides copper, iron, and trinkets, in the winter when the Indians were hungry, bread, rice, and molasses made good produce to barter. The products of one Indian group, such as tanned elk skins, would be picked up and traded to another group who wanted them. Advantage was taken of the Haida Indians' great luxury desire for the grease extracted from a small fish called shrow by the Nass River Indians. Thus, the *New Hazard* obtained a large amount of this grease, trading it for furs in the Queen Charlotte Islands. Slaves were purchased from one tribe and traded to another for skins. Commerce was also increasing between American ships and the Russian settlements in Alaska.

Results of the Northwest Coast–Pacific–China trade were lasting. The exploitation of natural resources changed the balance of nature in several parts of the world, for the slaughter of sea otters and seals and the overcutting of sandalwood was appalling. In New England not only do some of the fortunes made in the China trade still exist, in part at least, but, more important, profits from it served as a catalyst to later prosperity of the region, financing textile mills, shoe factories, and other industries, which in turn supplied the funds for many of our cultural institutions.

Another, permanent and delayed result to this early, almost wholly, New England exploitation of goods for the Canton market is even more evident. The decades of constant contact of American ships and traders, the sandalwooders and whalers, and finally the missionaries and educators, which in their day doubtless seemed of a most tenuous nature, created the atmosphere in the Hawaiian Islands that shaped their destiny as our fiftieth state.

17. Brig *New Hazard* of Salem

SEA OTTERS AND SANDALWOOD

IV ~

BÊCHE-DE-MER AND CANNIBALS

As the Hawaiian Islands became stripped of sandalwood, ships sought it farther afield in the Society Islands, Tonga, Samoa, and the Fijis. In the course of the search additional products of the islands were found to be desirable in China and other parts of the Far East. Two of these, tortoise shell and pearl shell, were used in China and India for manufacturing small items, for decorative work, and for inlay. Edible bird's-nest and *bêche-de-mer* made two of the Chinese's favorite soups. Thus a trader in the Central Pacific might load his vessel with a mixed cargo of sandalwood and other products.

The Boston Nor'west men did not dominate this new Pacific Islands trade. Bostonians had led the way to the Northwest Coast and the Hawaiian Islands. The whaling was dominated by Nantucket and New Bedford men, and the sealers came largely from the Connecticut shore. But it was the restless, enterprising merchants and captains from Boston's North Shore neighbor Salem, who earlier had pioneered the pepper trade in Sumatra, who now went to the Pacific for these other desirable products. Boston ships in general entered the Pacific around the Horn, but the Salem men preferred going by the Cape of Good Hope. From there it had been customary in the Far Eastern trade to head up through the Indian Ocean for India or to Sunda Straits and on to Manila or Canton. Many Salem captains preferred to go first to Australia or New Zealand, disposing of rum at Port Jackson (as Sydney was then called) or replenishing supplies at the Bay of Islands, as the whalers did, before continuing into the Central Pacific.

Trade centered on the Fiji group of more than two hundred islands, many of them large, lush, and a bountiful source of fresh provisions as well as trade products. In the warm waters surrounding the Fijis turtles and pearl shell thrived and bêche-de-mer abounded in enormous quantities.

Sandalwood first brought ships to Fiji. This aromatic wood was confined to what was then known as Sandalwood Island and is today called Vanua Levu, the second largest island of the Fijian group. Here along its southern coast sandalwood grew in profusion. The actual first contact between the Fijis and New England began in December 1799 when the Providence ship *Ann and Hope* touched briefly at Kadavu while on a voyage to Australia. As early as 1804 the *Fair American* of Boston got away with a full cargo from Sandalwood Bay. In 1806 Captain William Richardson of Salem arrived there to pick up a cargo of wood on his way to China. (His ship, the *Eliza,* is not to be confused with the ship *Eliza* from Providence which was wrecked in the Fijis in 1808.) In 1808 the *Jennie* of Boston, Captain William Dorr, arrived. His second mate was an Englishman, William Lockerby, who remained in the islands for two years, 1808 and 1809, and wrote a notable account of his activities there as a sandalwood trader and his life with the natives.[1]

BÊCHE-DE-MER AND CANNIBALS

During this time British Colonial ships from Australia were also trading in the Fijis and great rivalry developed between them and the New England vessels. Successive governors in New South Wales endeavored unsuccessfully to bar American ships from this trade. The warlike tendencies and independence of the Fijians themselves provided other difficulties. R. A. Derrick, the principal modern historian of the Fijis, has written:

For the natives, the sandalwood trade was probably the most injurious of all their early contact with white traders. It has been said that every stick of the wood had blood upon it. Chief vied with chief in laying claim to patches of trees that had suddenly become valuable; they drove their people to cut logs, quarrelling over the spoils. The natives generally were greedy to possess such new wealth as hoop-iron fashioned into crude chisels, or trade knives and axes; and when there was a chance of success they would attempt to rob or even murder traders to get these prized implements more easily. Outrages gave rise to reprisals, and generally the natives suffered more than the white.[2]

In February 1811 the Salem brig *Active,* commanded by Captain William Putnam Richardson (not the commander of the *Eliza*), cleared from Sydney in ballast for the Fijis and took on a full cargo of sandalwood logs. She accomplished this very quickly, for she left Fiji for Canton on July 21 of the same year, which indicates that the sandalwood trade in Fiji was well organized by this time. (Like the *Eliza,* the *Active* also touched at the Bay of Islands on her way to Fiji and both captains brought important ethnological collections back to Salem for the East India Marine Society's museum.) From the 1820's until the 1840's the bêche-de-mer trade was at its height, centering around the large island of Viti Levu, especially at Rewa and Mbau, where the most powerful chiefs lived.

For about forty years after the arrival of the Richardsons a series of noted and adventurous Salem captains did business in

18. Brig *Governor Endicott* of Salem

the Fiji Islands. Benjamin Vanderford, William Driver, John H. Eagleston, Benjamin Wallis, and many others made numerous voyages there. From 1821 to 1823 Captain Vanderford, who had been second mate under Richardson on the *Active,* took the brig *Roscoe* on a voyage which lasted thirty-two months and covered forty-five thousand miles from Salem to Tahiti, Samoa, the Fijis, New Hebrides, New Guinea, Manila, Batavia, Hamburg, Germany, and back to Salem. On the Fiji leg he loaded with sandalwood and also had a near mutiny on his hands. Stopping briefly at the New Hebrides, he gave presents to some natives and they returned his favor by shooting arrows

BÊCHE-DE-MER AND CANNIBALS

at him as his boat was pulling off from the shore. In Manila he unloaded the sandalwood and took on molasses and sugar; the sugar, along with camphor, mats, coffee, nankeens, and wax, was discharged in Hamburg. After the *Roscoe* voyage Vanderford continued in the trade as captain of the ship *Clay* owned by the Rogers brothers of Salem.

Of all the words one comes across in connection with South Sea trade, none is more evocative of romance and adventure than bêche-de-mer. But, while the word is familiar, few know

19. Brig *Leander* of Salem

NEW ENGLAND AND THE SOUTH SEAS

that bêche-de-mer is a holothurian, commonly called a sea slug or sea cucumber. Although this may be definite enough for identification, one can only visualize what the trade must have been like after seeing these animals in their native habitat. In 1957, in the Society Islands and in the Fijis, I had the opportunity to observe bêche-de-mer alive. After seeing in what enormous quantities these creatures abound in the shallow water around reefs, it is easy to imagine how a shipload could be obtained. The commonest variety, a small black species which varies from two to nine inches long, literally covers the bottom in places. There are stretches of sand between the coral heads where one can walk knee-deep for a mile or more and find it almost impossible not to step on these slimy, revolting animals. Besides the black variety, there are others much larger and far more decoratively colored. Different species are gray with red spots, striped yellow and black, dark brown or dirty white, and reddish; also smooth, with tubercles on the sides, or prickly. Their favorite habitat is on reefs where there is a mixture of sand and coral, commonly on the northern side of islands and only rarely on the southern coasts. The black kind resembles crepe in texture and apparently multiplies very fast, although it is said that in certain localities where the bêche-de-mer fishermen exterminated the creature it never returned in any numbers.

The Chinese, who regarded it as an aphrodisiac, greatly preferred some varieties to others; consequently there was a price differential. The Malays called bêche-de-mer trepang and one can still buy trepang soup in most good Chinese restaurants. The gray with red spots variety was eaten raw by the Fijians. The best animals for the trade were found in about two fathoms of water where they were collected by native divers. Another method of fishing was by torch or moonlight when the

BÊCHE-DE-MER AND CANNIBALS

creatures, crawling over the coral bottom like enormous caterpillars, came out in multitudes to suck in food.

Upon his arrival in the Fijis a captain first contacted a local chief and made arrangements to hire a gang of fishermen and erect a house in which to dry the product. The natives were paid with muskets, ammunition, whale's teeth, knives, scissors, chisels, hatchets, axes, plane iron, gouges, and fishhooks or small looking glasses, beads, trade cloth, and other knickknacks. Blue beads and cloth were preferred. One whale's tooth bought a hogshead of bêche-de-mer, and for a musket a hundred-fifty-gallon cask could be filled ten times.

Freshly collected bêche-de-mer could not be exposed to the sun lest they dissolve into a stringy mass. They had to be carefully covered until brought ashore for cleaning and drying. Once ashore, the fish, as they were called, were dumped into bins to drain. The bins, made of coconut logs set in trenches about two feet deep in the ground, held about forty or fifty hogsheads. Nearby were the trade houses where the natives were paid for the fish they collected. A ship's officer and a reliable seaman watched over the trade house and the bins. They sat on an elevated platform with a good view of everything taking place around them. After they had drained, a shallow incision was made in the side of each creature, which was then cleaned and spread open. They were next thrown into boiling caldrons of water—great, black, iron kettles identical to those used in the sugar bush of Vermont and somewhat smaller than the trypots of whalers. (These kettles occasionally are still found on island beaches of the South Seas.) Such sugar boilers, varying in size from one hundred to a hundred and fifty gallons, were propped up by stone and mud about two feet apart, with space beneath for a large fire. Work went on day and night with two men to each pot, provided with skimmers, ladles, fishhooks, hoes, and shovels. Fanning tells that in the boiling caldron was a strong pickle containing some saltpeter and a mite of alum which gave the bêche-de-mer a clear amber color and made it more desirable to the Chinese.[3] But Commodore Wilkes says that no water was put into the pots for the fish made their own liquor.[4] After boiling for twenty-five to fifty minutes and draining on the platform for an hour, they were ready for drying. The bêche-de-mer was laid about four inches deep on flakes in a dry shed, and in three or four days it was thoroughly cured.

The drying sheds were sometimes over a hundred feet long, fifteen or twenty feet wide, and twice as high. They had pitched roofs with gable ends, eaves coming down about five feet from the ground, and were well thatched and water-tight. A door at either end and another in the middle of one side gave easy access. Running the entire length of the inside was a row of double staging flakes, called batters. Captain Eagleston told Wilkes that much of the success of the undertaking depended on the construction of the staging.[5] The lower batter ran about four feet from the ground, with the upper two or three feet higher, and they were from twelve to fourteen feet wide. The batters were covered with large reeds woven together with small cords and upon these a fish fence was laid of smaller reeds. A trench was dug under the batters for a slow-burning fire which was cared for by natives under the direction of a ship's officer. All doors were kept shut during the drying and the house itself was always constructed at right angles to the course of the prevailing wind. The earth from the trench was thrown against the sides of the house to make it tighter and for fire prevention. As an additional precaution barrels of water were placed about eight feet apart on both sides of the batter. Heavy losses were sustained when drying houses burned. But, as after

BÊCHE-DE-MER AND CANNIBALS

a week's use they became almost explosive, once on fire there was no saving them. Charred parts were continually being replaced and while the drying was going on about fifteen men worked on the alert day and night. About once every twenty-four hours the fires were put out, the dried fish removed, and a new batch put in. The heat in an already hot climate made the work difficult, and in addition to the ship's men some fifty to sixty natives were usually employed for each house. Enormous quantities of firewood (purchased from the local chief at about twenty cords for a single musket) were used in the process. It required about half a cord of wood to cure each picul of bêche-de-mer.

20. Captain John H. Eagleston

21. Captain William Driver

The work was hard but the profits were enormous. In the course of his five voyages, the smallest lot of bêche-de-mer Captain John H. Eagleston collected was 617 piculs, which cost him $1,100 and sold for over $8,000. On his fifth, and most successful cruise, he collected 1200 piculs which cost $3,500 and sold for $27,000. On this same trip Captain Eagleston also collected 4488 pounds of tortoise shell at a cost of $5,700; instead of unloading it in the Far East market, he brought it back to the United States where it netted $29,050. It was profits of this kind that made men willing to risk their lives and ships in this precarious trade. One profitable voyage undertaken on margin could set a man up as a successful merchant.

If sufficient sandalwood, bêche-de-mer, and tortoise shell was not available, there was the pearl shell industry. To collect pearl shell, a gang of native divers was hired at a friendly island and taken to a pearl bank where the large oysters lay at the bottom in three or more fathoms of water. Each diver descended with a wicker basket weighted down with ten to twelve pounds of stone, as the depth of water might require. A coil of whale line was made fast to each basket and as the diver filled the basket with oysters he took out the stones. If he wished to come to the surface he yanked on the line and was quickly pulled up by men on deck. After recovering his breath he dove again. Considerable competition existed among the divers and each attempted to stay down the longest. Many were seriously injured and appeared on deck with eyes bulging and blood oozing from mouth, nose, and ears. The oysters were scraped, washed clean, and spread out in the hot sun to dry. After the oysters had been examined for pearls, the shell was dried, packed in casks or baskets, and stored in the vessel's holds. Once the hold had been filled, the natives were returned to their village and paid off. The chief was reimbursed according to the terms of the original bargain. Chinese merchants rated the pearl shell in five different qualities. The first "chop," as it was called, was the largest and purest pearl shell, most free from blemishes, which brought the highest price. The other four chops were scaled down in value according to the quality.

It has been said that Vanderford, who made a good many voyages to Fiji after his first trip on the *Active,* and William Driver, who was his first mate in the ship *Clay* in the middle 1820's, were the first white men to cure a full cargo of bêche-de-mer in the islands. However, small lots of bêche-de-mer were collected before that time. Vanderford himself was there in the ship *Indus* for sandalwood between 1817 and 1820 and no doubt took some bêche-de-mer with him then. He was there again in the *Roscoe* in 1821 for both products, but by that time there was little sandalwood left. Because of the many dangerous reefs that abounded in the uncharted waters of Fiji, wrecks were not unusual. Among the Salem vessels that left their bones in the Fijis were the whaler *Oeno,* all of whose men but one were slain by the Fijians; the *Glide,* which had two men killed before she was wrecked; the *Niagara* and *Fawn,* both wrecked and looted; and the *Charles Doggett,* which also ran aground and had several of her crew killed.

The case of the *Glide* is the best documented. She was owned by Joseph Peabody of Salem and sailed for the South Pacific on May 22, 1829, under Captain Henry Archer. Upon his arrival in the Fijis in October, Archer established his trade rates. For a common musket they obtained a dozen large hogs; for a pair of scissors or a jackknife, a bunch of plantains and from thirty to forty coconuts. (From a sailor's point of view one of the advantages of the trade was the bountiful supplies. Everyone lived well.) Shortly after her arrival, the *Glide* ran in with the brig *Quill,* Captain Joshua Kinsman of Salem, with William Driver as his first mate. After the natives had bartered everything stockpiled in their village—mats, tortoiseshell,

22. Ship *Glide* of Salem

hogs, and vegetables for the iron tools, knives, scissors, whales'
teeth, beads, and especially muskets and ammunition—they
would consent to collect and cure bêche-de-mer. While collecting his cargo of "fish" Captain Archer was also successful
in obtaining several hundred pounds of tortoise shell.

On January 30, with the *Glide* about a third loaded,
Captain Archer had his batter house burned and boiling
kettles broken by the natives. He then took possession of the
buildings that had recently been used by Kinsman of the *Quill,*
who had taken a full cargo off to Manila. In April he learned
that the ship *Clay* with Captain Millet from Salem was also
in the islands. On April 15 the *Glide* ran onto a reef, but was
gotten off with great difficulty. A few days later she sailed for
Manila with a thousand piculs of bêche-de-mer, three hundred

BÊCHE-DE-MER AND CANNIBALS

pounds of tortoise shell, and seven hundred pounds of sandal-wood. Disposing of his cargo and returning to the Fijis by way of the Hawaiian Islands and Penrhyn Island, Captain Archer learned that the brig *Fawn* had been lost. While eight of the *Glide's* men were ashore getting a new anchor stock they were attacked by natives and two sailors, Joshua Derby and Enoch Knight, were killed. Their bodies, stripped of clothing and dreadfully mangled, were later recovered from the beach. Captain Archer traded along the coast, visited King Tanoa at Mbau, and as a diversion had a group of his men put on a play for the Fijians about the Fiji trade, which amused the natives very much.

On March 21 a gale arose which developed into a hurricane. The ship dragged her anchors and, although the captain had her masts cut away, she continued toward the reef where she piled up a few minutes after ten o'clock the next morning. As the rocks broke through her, the water rushed into her hold. The men, saving a few supplies, got ashore. The natives took over the ship and eventually burned her for her iron. Most of the *Glide's* crew survived and were scattered throughout the Pacific on various vessels; many of them had extraordinary adventures and did not get back to Salem for years.

No captain was more accomplished in the bêche-de-mer trade than John Henry Eagleston who made several successful voyages between 1830 and 1840 for Stephen C. Phillips of Salem. The bark *Peru* and the ship *Emerald* were two of his most successful commands, and he became well-known and influential among the Fijian chiefs. It was he who christened one of the Mbau chiefs Phillips after his employer. It was he also who brought the first cattle to Fiji and called them "bulamacow," a term used by the natives ever since.

Eagleston had many scraps with the natives and was always on the alert against their treachery, but he did not allow another captain to outwit him. The bêche-de-mer trade was a cutthroat business, and, although most of the captains were Salem neighbors, they oftentimes tried to barter for fish from the natives which had already been gathered for a competitor. Eagleston and Vanderford had a monumental row, threatening to fire on each other's ships, over jurisdiction of a certain bêche-de-mer reef; they detested each other ever after.

The best-documented voyages to the Fijis are the last two of Captain Benjamin Wallis near the end of the bêche-de-mer trade. Captain Wallis of Beverly, who had married Mary Davis Cook of the same town, was master of the bark *Zotoff* of Salem. He took this ship, nicknamed "Old Soft-tack" by the sailors, on four voyages to the Fijis. On the last two voyages between 1844 to 1850 his wife accompanied him. Her book, entitled *Life In Fiji,* is a notable account of the trade, of the natives, of canni-balism, and of the heroic efforts of the missionaries during that time.[6] Mrs. Wallis describes

23. Captain Benjamin Wallis

them with an objective point of view. Her day-to-day adven-tures now seem almost incredible, for even at that late date the brutality and ruthlessness of the natives was appalling.

In 1840, when Captain Charles Wilkes was in the Fijis with

the United States Exploring Expedition, he not only received advice from Captain Eagleston about getting one of his ships inside a reef, but he had with him as pilot Eagleston's rival, Benjamin Vanderford, who died on the voyage and was buried at sea.

The gathering of edible bird's-nest so desired by the Chinese also required a special technique. The nests are built by swifts with an excretion which comes from their mouths in the form of a sort of gummy thread of white or clear amber color. A yellow or black variety was of less value. The nests were gathered from clefts along the rocky coast by two men in a boat. One, armed with a small billhook secured to a pole ten or eighteen feet long, hooked off the nests, while the man with a scoop-net about the size of a barrelhead caught them as they fell. When a boatload was secured, the feathers and dirt were carefully removed and, after the nests were dried in the sun, they were packed in boxes lined with mats of thick paper as protection against dampness and were ready for the market. Like bêche-de-mer bird's-nest could be ruined if they got wet in passage, for they would then become soft and moldy. The quantity of nests was never large and, therefore, the price was high. Only the wealthiest Chinese could afford to eat the bird's-nest soup or serve it at their tables.

The South Sea trade was a dangerous one. Dangerous, because most of the islands around which the ships worked were poorly charted, or not charted at all. Coral reefs, with the dangerous coral heads sometimes but a few inches below the surface, were a constant danger.

Aside from natural hazards, the natives themselves were an uncertain element, and in no group of islands was this more true than the Fijis. The Fiji Islanders were the most unpredictable, the most savage customers, the traders had to deal with. They were also the greatest cannibals in the period from about 1800 to 1850. Nowhere else in the world were so many people slaughtered and eaten. The warring natives ate their enemies as a matter of course, but the practice became so flagrant that everyone was in danger.

One of the worst promoters of this wretched custom was a survivor of the brig *Eliza* from Providence, which was wrecked in 1808 on a reef before reaching Sandalwood Bay. He was a tough seaman named Charles Savage who made himself the leader of a prime collection of renegade sailors, beachcombers, and escaped convicts who were already trickling into the islands. Savage and the beachcombers ushered in a new era, a period of muskets and civil wars, of rebellions, invasions, and massacres, that reached its height at the time when the bêche-de-mer traders were trying to cure their cargoes. Small wonder that it took bold men with steady nerves and instincts for self-preservation as well as trade to enter the bêche-de-mer business!

Surrounded by this "palace guard" armed with firearms salvaged from the *Eliza,* Savage attached himself to old Tanoa, the principal chief at the island of Mbau, as advisor and mercenary. As intelligent as he was hard-boiled, Savage learned the native language, took all the best looking women for his harem, and provided the Mbauian warriors with firearms. He achieved a dubious fame, by becoming the first man to introduce firearms to Fiji and teaching the natives to use them. For, following this, the raiding which had always gone on between the various Fijian chiefs became incessant and the slaughter incredible. Savage's tattooed white riffraff, a depraved lot who were regarded with some alarm even by the cannibals, backed the Mbauians who soon gained the reputation of being the greatest warriors in the islands. Now there were bodies aplenty for eating and the common people rapidly developed a taste and craving for "long pig." Savage finally made his mistake. He attempted to get a cargo of sandalwood from the natives without paying for it. The Fijians did not take kindly to the double cross, an art in which they were expert. Six men held Savage's head in a well until he drowned. He was eaten and his bones made into sail needles which were distributed among the people. He and his gang of renegade whites were eliminated, but under their influence cannibalism deteriorated from a religious practice, conducted with formality and a certain amount of restraint, to a fearful orgiastic nightmare.

Charles Savage was only one of a number of white men in Fiji at this time, but he was one of the worst. One of the best was David Whippey, a native of Nantucket, who deserted from a whale ship, lived there the rest of his life, and built the first vessel ever constructed in Fiji. He acquired great influence among the natives, and acted as an interpreter and negotiator between them and traders and missionaries. He took a native wife and was a stabilizing influence in the islands. But not until the Fijis were turned over to the British Crown by Thakombau, October 10, 1874, could it be said that real law and order came to the cannibal islands. Thakombau had been for some years, in fact, the fabulous king of the cannibal isles— inspiration of the jokes of the last hundred years showing cannibals simmering a white man in a big black pot. Actually, long pig was usually cooked in great stone ovens, but the black sugar boilers for curing bêche-de-mer were put to the far more horrible use on at least one occasion.

Thakombau and his father, old Tanoa, were but two of a

number of prominent chiefs with whom the traders did business. They are, however, the most important and perhaps best examples of the kind of men the Salem adventurers had to deal with. Tanoa was a notorious butcher and despot who needed no excuse—such as war or revenge—in order to kill, but slaughtered his own subjects for sport and food. As a youth Thakombau witnessed the wiping out of an entire subject community of 1800 people who were killed and distributed for food. When Tanoa launched his great war canoes, instead of rollers he laid men side by side and slid the heavy, hundred-foot-long boats over their bodies into the water. When one of his cousins gave him some offense he walked up to the relative and kissed him, and then cut off his arm and tossed it into the fire. Following this, he had his kinsman taken apart limb by limb and eaten. When one of his subjects stole some yams

24. Thakombau as a young man

BÊCHE-DE-MER AND CANNIBALS

from the king and disappeared with the loot, Tanoa ruled, "Take his father and kill him, it makes no difference."[7] With such exhibitions Tanoa trained his most promising son to be the greatest cannibal that ever lived, encouraging Thakombau to kill his own brother. Thakombau grew into a six-foot-six, bushy-headed, black-bearded, heavily muscled native.

As the popularity of cannibalism spread among the people no one knew from one day to the next when he might be clubbed and eaten. A shipwrecked sailor might be knocked on the head, women going for food or water waylaid, friends invited for feasts treacherously killed, or people seized at random because a chief wanted meat. The Reverend Thomas Williams recorded an extraordinary case concerning a Fijian commoner known as Loti, who, with no other motive than his fondness for human flesh, killed and ate his only wife after she had finished planting taro and collected enough wood to make a fire.[8] The ovens, pots, and dishes used for cooking and eating human flesh were taboo for other purposes. Long pig was said to leave a phosphorescence on the hands which glowed after dark and, therefore, it was only eaten with a special wooden fork,* never used for any other food.[9] Only men were allowed to eat human flesh, although after a feast the women and children sometimes surreptitiously cleaned the bones.

In 1832 a group of lesser chiefs at Mbau were involved in a bloodless uprising—no common thing in Fiji—against King Tanoa, who was forced to flee into exile. The victorious chiefs decided that Thakombau, who was only seventeen years old, could live, as he was a harmless boy. This was their downfall. The boy carried on a gay masquerade of spending his time

* Thakombau's personal cannibal fork is now on exhibition at the Peabody Museum of Salem.

fishing, eating, drinking, and sleeping, but all the while he was plotting a careful counterrevolution which would restore his father to power. He had a nucleus of strength in a community of loyal fishermen and a few chiefs who lived along the waterfront. Laying his plans slowly and carefully, he achieved a successful coup in 1837, which allowed his father to return to Mbau in triumph. As soon as Tanoa's power was re-established he put a bounty on the heads of all rebels and ordered his son to exterminate them. The rebels' friends turned them over to Thakombau for the head price, and he gave them to the fishermen to eat. Tanoa was restored to power, but his son's success in accomplishing that feat gave the young man great prestige. Thakombau now overshadowed his father as the most important man in Mbau, even though his father continued as the nominal head chief for many years. From this time on it was Thakombau who ran the government, made the decisions, and bargained with traders, sea captains, and missionaries.

The isolated island of Mbau can be visited today only by canoe or by walking at low tide over the mudflats from the peaceful coastal village of Somo Somo. It is difficult to reconcile the quiet scene with the shocking practices common in the time of Thakombau and the New England traders. The year of his father's return from exile was a momentous one in another way for the young chief. One day, just as Thakombau and his chiefs were dining on one of the rebels with two others roasting in the oven nearby, two missionaries, the Reverend William Cross and his helper the Reverend David Cargill, arrived. Cross was the head of the Wesleyan mission, and as Mbau was the most important town in the islands he thought it would be the appropriate place to establish his head-quarters.

BÊCHE-DE-MER AND CANNIBALS

In answer to the missionaries' request Thakombau said, "it will be most agreeable to me if you think well, but I will not hide it from you that I am now engaged in war and cannot attend to your instruction or even insure you of safety."[10] In the face of this, Cross decided that, as there was little prospect of security or success at Mbau, he should establish the mission at Rewa, the second largest town in the islands, where Thakombau's brother-in-law was chief. This decision, which seemed a wise one at the time, may have set back the Christianizing of the Fijis for a quarter of a century. At the time of Cross's visit Thakombau was not opposed to Christianity. His reply granting permission even without protection was a condescension on his part. His further implication that he would attend instruction if he had time was even more astonishing. If Cross had been more familiar with the country and the ways of Fijian chiefs he would have taken in the full purport of the reply and probably would have settled in Mbau. As it was, his failure to do so gave Thakombau great offense and made him the unremitting enemy of the missionary efforts for many years to come.

Two years later, in 1839, Cross decided the time was ripe to transfer to the Fijian capital. His approach this time was through Tanoa who attempted to put him off diplomatically by saying, "The island is small, the people foolish. I fear they will take your property from you. Water and firewood are difficult to obtain." [11] Cross was not discouraged by these difficulties and put the matter bluntly to Thakombau, at the same time upbraiding him for his cannibalism and other vices. This missionary's personality and zeal was such that he inevitably succeeded in irritating the great chief. Thakombau exploded and stated flatly that he would always oppose Christianity, and that none of his family should ever become converted if he could prevent it. His parting remark at Cross was, "When you have grown taro on yon bare rock, then will I become a Christian and not before." Cross departed, observing that, "Thakombau has all the cruelty of his father and is far superior in his war-like ability." In the years that followed Thakombau considered the destruction of all Fijian Christians and annoyed the missionaries who had settled in other towns in every ingenious way he could contrive. To one of his chiefs, who in his opinion was becoming too friendly toward the missionaries, he remarked, "Wonderful is the new religion is it not, but will it prevail? Will it prevent our having men to eat? Not it." [12]

In 1840 Commodore Charles Wilkes with the United States Exploring Expedition arrived in the Fijis. Inviting Thakombau aboard his flagship *Vincennes,* he gave him some firm advice. Wilkes describes the young cannibal as "extremely good-looking, being tall, well-made and athletic. He exhibits much intelligence, both in his expression, countenance, and manners. His features and figure resemble those of a European and he is graceful and easy in his carriage." He failed to show the hauteur and arrogant bearing for which he was noted, but rather appeared simply, "young and frisky." Thakombau was particularly impressed with the firing of the ship's guns and requested Wilkes to fire them again. Upon being presented with a musket, he dismantled it with the expertness of a gunsmith and reassembled it again.[13] He was definitely on his good behavior. A few days later in Wilkes's absence Thakombau visited the ship again and exhibited some of his less lovable traits. He behaved in an insolent and presumptuous manner and succeeded in stealing the personal belongings of one of the expedition's pilots. Possibly he may have been brooding over a recent row with the chief of a neighboring island from whom he had tried unsuccessfully to collect a quantity of coconut oil. The vassal chief explained that it had been a physical impossibility to have the large amount of oil ready in the specified time. Thakombau called him a liar and without further discussion clubbed and killed him on the spot.

Having pacified Mbau and cowed the missionaries by 1840, Thakombau was ready to attempt to subdue the rest of the Fijis. For the next decade, following the time-honored custom of allying himself with the weaker of two opponents (which by intrigue he had already incited to war), he would defeat his stronger rival and then attack his ally. During this period he achieved his notoriety for treachery, ruthlessness, and cruelty.

Thakombau's successes were sufficient for him to begin calling himself King of Fiji, which he did, although his father was still living. Subject villages regularly sent him tribute of coconut oil, whales' teeth, slaves, and whatever else he desired. As his conquests spread and his goal of becoming ruler of all Fiji grew near, Thakombau began to be more selective in his trading with whites. He refused to accept the usual trade cloth and stores for native products, and insisted on receiving fire-arms, lead, powder, and rum. He claimed to have five thousand muskets, one thousand kegs of powder, pigs of lead, and bullet molds of American manufacture capable of running a dozen balls at a time. With his success his reputation for personal bravery, courage, and ferocity in war increased. He even com-mitted an act of clemency when he spared the life of an enemy he had run through with a spear.

Thakombau was now nearing the peak of his power. If a town offended him he killed a score of men in vengeance and brought the canoes loaded with corpses to Mbau to hand out to his people. He became more arrogant with white traders and missionaries. In a generous moment he presented Captain

Benjamin Wallis, a Salem trader, with a cow. A few days later the Captain politely invited his Majesty to dine on board the bark *Zotoff* and offered him some beef soup. Thakombau whimsically declined to taste it, saying that the cow was born at Mbau, he had seen her walking about and eating the grass of the island, and he loved her, therefore, he could not eat a portion of her body.

25. Bark *Zotoff* of Salem

Dealing with this kind of man, and the lesser chiefs were for the most part different only in degree, kept the New Englanders alert. Eventually, because of the work of the mission-

BÊCHE-DE-MER AND CANNIBALS

aries and the menacing visits of English and American warships
which arrived to protect their nationals, Thakombau saw that
his time was up. He was an astute thinker, however, and,
becoming converted to Christianity, took the biblical name of

26. Thakombau in old age

Ebenezer. In 1858, in order to clear up the many debts he had
brought upon himself by indiscriminately purchasing gun-
boats and other warlike material, he ceded the Fiji Islands to
Queen Victoria as a Crown Colony, but they were not accepted
until 1874. So, from the early 1800's, at about the time when
the William Richardsons first arrived, until long after the last
of the New England traders had departed, Thakombau and
his father were the dominant personalities of the islands.

New England trade in the Fijis may be divided roughly into two parts. The sandalwood trade was the earlier; it began about 1800, and by 1815 all the sandalwood had been cut. The bêche-de-mer trade did not become a major commercial undertaking until about 1822. One of the interesting differences between the two was the fact that the vessels in the sandalwood trade hailed from a number of ports, while the bêche-de-mer trade was confined almost entirely to Salem ships.

The local character of the bêche-de-mer trade, centering as it did on Salem, prevented it from assuming the importance in the over-all New England economy of the sea otter, seal, and sandalwood aspects of the China commerce. Nevertheless, bêche-de-mer and the Fijis contributed handsomely to the prosperity of Massachusetts in the first half of the nineteenth century.

BÊCHE-DE-MER AND CANNIBALS

27. Hawaiian dancing

V ~

WITH COURAGE AND ZEAL

In 1957, at the remote phosphate island of Makatea shortly after our C-2 freighter *Pioneer Reef* tied up to the buoys to discharge oil, I was astonished to be greeted by a young man, half-Tahitian, half-French, who said he had visited the Peabody Museum in Salem a few years before when he came to Gloucester to help sail several fishing schooners back to the South Seas. Later at Papeete I met two other Tahitians who had taken part in the same expedition. It was one of the fates of able, Gloucester sailing fishermen to end up in the South Seas as native trading schooners.

These Polynesians continued a tradition of visits by South Seas Islanders to New England that had its beginnings in the late eighteenth century. Captain Amasa Delano in 1801 brought back a young Hawaiian who was "much admired by the audience and the publick in general." Even earlier than that, a Hawaiian named Attoo had returned with Captain Robert Gray on his circumnavigation with the ship *Columbia*. Attoo also was admired in Boston where, dressed in a feather cloak and helmet acquired by Gray, he attracted enormous attention.

Attoo was the first of many South Sea Island sailors. The Polynesians were curious to see the wonders of the world with which the seamen filled their ears, and many of them shipped on American vessels. They made good seamen and could be hired cheaply. Considerable scandal was caused at one period when unscrupulous captains on the slightest pretext let their more undesirable crew members go and shipped Hawaiians instead. The whalers, sandalwood and bêche-de-mer traders in Fiji, the Societies, and New Zealand frequently had one or more natives aboard. Sometimes more than half the crew came from the islands. The Maoris of New Zealand acquired a particular reputation as harpooners, as did some of the Marquesans.

No Polynesian who visited New England more influenced the later history of his islands, albeit indirectly, than the Hawaiian Opukahaia, or Obookiah, as he was more generally known. When Henry Obookiah, to give him his baptismal name, was about twelve years old he saw his father and mother killed in a local feud. The orphan was looked after by his uncle, a priest of the native Hawaiian religion, who instructed him in its practices. In 1808, when he was sixteen years old, he was brought to the United States by a New Haven shipmaster. The following year the Reverend Edwin W. Dwight, it is said, found him lonely and weeping on the steps of one of the Yale buildings. Dwight befriended the homeless boy and began to instruct him in Christianity. Shortly thereafter Obookiah attracted the attention of Mr. Samuel J. Mills whose father was a Congregational minister in Torrington, Connecticut. He lived in the Mill's home where he was educated by the clergyman and worked on his farm.

The American Board of Commissioners for Foreign Missions was founded in 1810, and Obookiah, stimulated by Samuel Mills who was interested in foreign missions, inspired them to found the Foreign Mission school at Cornwall, Connecticut, in 1817. The school was established for the specific purpose of training young natives in Christianity, so that they might become missionaries to their homelands. Five of the first ten pupils in the school were Hawaiians. Unfortunately Obookiah died on February 17, 1818, when he was twenty-six years old and still in training, but the published account of his life[1] stimulated further interest in sending missionaries to the Pacific.

About this time Hiram Bingham, a young student at Andover (Massachusetts) Theological Seminary, offered to go as a missionary to the Hawaiian Islands. He was joined by his classmate, Asa Thurston, who was a graduate of Yale College and one of her great athletes. Their offer was enthusiastically accepted by the American Board.

On October 15, 1819, a public meeting was held in the Park Street Church at Brimstone Corner in Boston. Bingham and Thurston were now ordained ministers. They had also gotten married, for the Board had decided that only married men should be sent as missionaries to the islands.* Others joining the first two volunteers were Thomas Holman, a physician; Samuel Whitney and Samuel Ruggles, schoolteachers; Elisha

*Asa Thurston barely made it. Shortly after this ruling was announced he visited an aunt and expressed fear that he would not be allowed to go unless he could find a wife. The aunt had a relative who was also interested in missions. This girl was Lucy Goodale, whom Asa married within a few weeks. They were destined to live the rest of their lives in the Hawaiian Islands, where Lucy Goodale Thurston became one of the Islands' grand old ladies.

Loomis, a printer; and Daniel Chamberlain, a farmer—all with their wives. Three of the young Hawaiians who had attended the Cornwall school—Thomas Hopu, William Kanui, and John Honolii—were also thought ready to return to their native land.

This missionary enterprise to Hawaii of New England Calvinism created enormous interest. Over five hundred people attended a special service the following Sunday at Park Street Church, and on Saturday morning October 23, a great crowd assembled at Long Wharf to bid farewell to the little expedition. Thomas Hopu, who had delivered a sermon on October 15, spoke again to the crowd after prayers had been offered, and the group sang "Blest be the tie that binds" and "When shall we meet again." The American Board had chartered the brig *Thaddeus* for the voyage and the missionary group was ferried aboard by a barge from the U.S.S. *Independence*. After the touching farewell, Captain Andrew Blanchard weighed anchor.

During the next thirty-five years twelve other contingents of missionaries were sent out to the Hawaiian Islands by the American Board. In these groups were many names that became famous in Hawaii. The second group had Lorrin Andrews who compiled the first Hawaiian dictionary; Peter J. Gulick, one of a famous clerical family; Gerrit P. Judd the physician, later so influential in government matters in Honolulu. Sheldon Dibble the historian was in the third expedition; another historian, William P. Alexander, was in the fourth, along with John S. Emerson and David D. Lyman. It is said of these missionaries that they "came to Hawaii to do good and did well," and of some that is true, for their names are still among the leading families of Hawaii.

NEW ENGLAND AND THE SOUTH SEAS

Leaving the *Thaddeus* to beat her way around the Horn, let us precede her to where extraordinary things were happening. The great king Kamehameha I, who had succeeded in consolidating his rule over the entire Hawaiian group, died May 8, 1819 at the age of eighty-two. He had been a firm old pagan and a strong advocate of the native Hawaiian religion with its elaborate taboo system.* Only the year before his death three men had been sacrificed at Kealakekua Bay for violation of a taboo. Kamehameha's power was absolute and none of his subjects had questioned his authority. Below the surface, however, there was considerable dissatisfaction with the old religion. Many of the leading chiefs and some of the priests had ceased to believe in the powers of the ancient deities. Much of this was due to the fact that for years they had watched white men, sailors and traders, violate the taboos with no ill effects. Among the chiefs' wives, especially, there was unrest, for the taboos weighed more heavily on the women than on the men. Many of the more desirable kinds of food were forbidden to women, and there had long been secret plotting between two of the principal queens for the abolition of the oppressive system. The entire native religious structure was ready to crumble, as it did shortly after the iron hand of Kamehameha I was removed.

Within two weeks of the death of Kamehameha, Liholiho was given the sovereign power and took the name of Kamehameha II at a ceremony before a vast crowd of chiefs, warriors, and common people. He was a handsome man; and, dressed in his cocked hat and feather cloak, attended by chiefs

*Near the end of his life it was said that Kamehameha heard about certain changes which were taking place in the Society Islands. He inquired about the nature of this new Christian religion but was unable to find anyone to answer his questions satisfactorily.

in feather helmets and mantles, and surrounded by attendants carrying magnificent plumed kahilis, he was an impressive sight.

Liholiho, however, was a dissolute prince without his father's attributes of greatness. The two queens, Keopuolani and Kaahumanu, knew the young man well and decided to do away with the taboo system once and for all. At the coronation ceremony Kaahumanu came to meet him and publicly declared that it was his father's will that he should be king but that she should rule jointly with him and have equal authority. She proposed that the taboos be disregarded,

28. A morai at Kealakekua, Hawaii

but the young king, brought up in the traditions of his people, was hesitant. He remembered that the last injunction of his father was on no account to forsake the old religion. That evening, Keopuolani, the queen mother, had the king's younger brother come and eat with her in defiance of the taboo;

NEW ENGLAND AND THE SOUTH SEAS

although Liholiho permitted it, he did not violate the taboo himself. Shortly thereafter he attempted to consecrate two native heiaus or temples but, because of general drunkenness and disorder, botched the proceedings.

When Liholiho returned to Kailua, Kaahumanu again requested him to renounce the native religion. This time the king listened to her wishes. He and his party embarked in several canoes and spent two days in drunken revelry, during which time he violated the taboo several times. When he arrived at Kailua a great feast was prepared and he and all the chiefs and their wives sat down and ate together openly. This was strictly against the Hawaiian religion, and multitudes of common people looked on with fear and curiosity to see what judgment the gods would call down upon their leaders for so impious an act. When no harm resulted the crowd cheered. The gods were dead and the taboo system was gone forever. The High Chief, himself, set an example by setting fire to the idols, and messengers were sent throughout the island to proclaim the abolition of the taboos. Revelry and license prevailed, but there was one last ditch fight. The conservative element rallied around and raised an army to restore the old gods but they were defeated in a battle fought December 20, 1819. Following the battle, all of the wooden figures and sacred enclosures, with few exceptions, were destroyed, and Hawaii presented to the world the strange spectacle of a nation without a religion.[2]

The timing of these circumstances could not have been more fortuitous for the missionary effort. The *Thaddeus* arrived at Kailua, Hawaii, on March 30, 1820, and the pioneer missionaries learned with astonishment that Kamehameha was dead and that the old religion had been repudiated. Only in remote hamlets and isolated regions of the islands did the

ancient beliefs and practices cling. For all that, Liholiho was
reluctant to allow the missionaries to reside in the islands.
His British advisers argued that if he permitted American
missionaries to stay they would plot to have the islands taken
over politically by the United States. Only when he was
assured that he need not permit the missionaries to stay
indefinitely did he rather grudgingly consent to their residence
for a year in the islands. With that consent the Thurstons and
Dr. and Mrs. Thomas Holman decided to stay at Kailua and
start their work at that place, while the *Thaddeus* continued
on to Honolulu.

29. Early view of the Hawaiian Islands

Honolulu was destined to be the most important mission
post, and the leadership of the entire missionary effort was
jealously guarded by the Reverend Hiram Bingham. This
leadership, for which he was in many ways admirably qualified,
was entirely unofficial as far as the American Board was

concerned, and more than one of his colleagues privately resented it. He was, however, a stubborn, intelligent, and courageous man, unswerving in his devotion to New England Calvinism. The missionaries brought the rigid moral code of New England Puritans to the islands with them. They insisted on strict observance of the Sabbath, the doctrines of original sin, and the sufficiency of the Scriptures.

From a religious point of view the missionaries had entered a vacuum, yet it was not easy to impose the rigid code of New England sexual morality upon the gay Polynesians. The devotion and fortitude of most of these clergymen and their families during the early years of their efforts is remarkable, for it was several years before they made much headway. Sensibly they devoted themselves first to mastering the rather simple language, but by 1824 the mission was firmly established. In October of that year they undertook to translate the Bible into Hawaiian, a formidable task which was completed in March 1839, after fourteen years of tedious work in which several of the men cooperated.

While the American Board of Commissioners was somewhat niggardly in sending supplies, books, and equipment to its people in the field, it sent a continuous stream of reinforcements. From the fourteen adults who arrived in 1820, the mission grew to more than fifty men and women by 1832, and it included men who had a diversity of knowledge that was helpful to the natives.

Considering their small numbers, their accomplishments in a relatively short time were a tribute to their tenacity and capacity for hard work. The first elementary speller in Hawaiian came from the mission press in January 1822. Before this it had been necessary to reduce the language to writing, no small achievement. The king became interested in this novelty and insisted that he should be the first one taught to read and write in his own language, but his habits were such that he made little headway. Nevertheless, he encouraged his chiefs and the important people in the kingdom to accept instruction, and this example of the aristocracy encouraged the commoners to do likewise. A year later it was said that there were more than two hundred pupils in schools which had been established upon the islands of Oahu and Kauai. In 1823 the English missionary Reverend William Ellis lent his support to the Americans. By 1829 at least forty-five thousand Hawaiians were receiving instruction in over seven hundred schools; and, while the attendance may have been irregular and the general enthusiasm for learning not too great, this is a remarkable achievement for it represents about 40 percent of all the Hawaiian population at that time.

While the missionaries did not have to contend with pagan priests, many factors complicated their efforts. Not the least was the trait of Polynesian character which desires to please. There is no doubt that some of the efforts to read and write and probably a good deal of the attendance at services were a combination of curiosity and pleasing the missionaries whom they liked, for the missionaries represented a civilization and way of life which the Hawaiians admired. Most of the foreign population, especially the traders, did not like the missionaries, although in general they were polite to them. The enormous profits made by the traders in sandalwood, for instance, dropped considerably, for the missionaries insisted, inasmuch as they were able, in getting fair treatment for the Hawaiians. They were unswerving in their efforts to prevent the natives from being cheated, and this was resented by the more unscrupulous traders. The whalers did not like the imposition of puritan moral standards upon the natives, for no longer did the Polynesian women come aboard their ships.

The missionaries fortunately were aided by having the almost immediate sympathy and assistance of many of the chiefs and their wives. One of the most fortunate circumstances occurred when Keopuolani, the king's mother, after her removal to Lahaina became the first person to be baptized on the island. The ceremony was performed by Reverend William

30. Honolulu

Ellis, and occurred not long before she died on September 16, 1823. She became quite a devout Christian, her behavior contrasting strongly with her proud heathen days. She had always been an amiable, mild-mannered person, but, before her conversion, whenever she walked abroad her subjects fell prostrate. She left orders that on her death no heathen ceremony should be practiced.

Another of the great women chiefs, Kapiolani, ruled over

WITH COURAGE AND ZEAL

large possessions in the neighborhood of Captain Cook's old haven at Kealakekua Bay. She and her husband requested a missionary for their village and erected a building for him. She made an enormous impression on her subjects when, in 1825, she journeyed one hundred miles to the crater of Kilauea where Pele, the volcano goddess, lived. Her entire journey with her retinue was made on foot. At the volcano, she ate the ohelo berries sacred to Pele and which were taboo without the goddess' permission. When she reached the crater she went down the steep path and across the lava beds, where steam issued from the crevices. Before her was the lake of fire, into which she hurled stones—the most disrespectful and displeasing thing she could do to the goddess. She concluded this remarkable performance of insults by turning to her followers and saying, "Jehovah is my God. He kindled these fires. I fear not Pele," and so on. Whereupon, the entire company knelt in prayer and sang a hymn.[3]

Most of the powerful chiefs were responsive to the teachings of the missionaries with the exception of the king himself. After the death of his mother Keopuolani, he boasted to the Russian explorer, Otto von Kotzebue, that he was a Christian, but he never really became one. In November 1823 the king took passage on a whaler to visit his royal colleague, George IV. Both he and his wife died of measles in England.

Late in 1825, Kaahumanu, the old widow of the great Kamehameha I and now regent of the young Kamehameha III, and nine principal chiefs were admitted to the Church as members in full communion. They were followed by encouraging numbers of commoners. This more or less officially established Christianity as the religion of the islands. But such a demonstration of public fervor did not mean that all the Hawaiians had suddenly been turned into Polynesian counterparts of New England Puritans. So ingrained was the custom among the Hawaiians of obeying the slightest hint of their chiefs that, when the queen regent Kaahumanu became converted, it was natural for the common people to do likewise. This enthusiasm for religion continued until her death in 1832, and during that period the church in Honolulu was thronged every Sunday morning by congregations numbering from three to four thousand Hawaiians. The missionaries became desperate for books in sufficient numbers and for teachers. In many cases the native teachers, who were instructing their fellow countrymen to read and write, were hardly more advanced than their pupils. Nevertheless, while there was a return to vice and violence after the queen regent's death and during the remainder of the dissolute reign of Kamehameha III, the missionaries had acquired enormous influence in the islands. Sundays were quiet and even efforts to promote temperance and chastity slowly gained headway, for many of the converts made serious attempts to regulate their lives by strict New England standards.

An extraordinary manifestation of missionary success occurred in late 1836 with the beginning of the Great Revival which reached its peak in 1838 and 1839. Hawaiians flocked by the thousands to join the Church and were taken in. In the autumn of 1838 a congregation estimated at at least ten thousand natives assembled on the western shore of the island of Hawaii to hear the preaching of the Gospel. The enormous congregations required large meeting houses. One thatched building was built at Kailua big enough to hold nearly five thousand people. It measured one hundred and eighty feet long, seventy-eight feet broad, and covered fourteen thousand square feet. Hiram Bingham addressed congregations of two or three thousand, and natives flocked to meetings in even greater numbers on Hawaii. Schools had been established in every district of the islands, with some four hundred teachers, nearly all natives, and twenty-five thousand pupils, mostly adults. With the Great Revival it can be safely said that the missionaries had succeeded in their unrelaxed effort to transfer the religious, social, and moral ideals of New England to the Hawaiian Islands.

The year 1826 marks the beginning of another aspect of the missionary efforts in the Hawaiian Islands. Reverend Ellis, who had been so helpful to the Americans, was forced to return to England in 1822 because of his wife's health. He suggested to the American Board of Commissioners for Foreign Missions that a small schooner should be built and sent to the islands for the use of workers in the field for interisland travel. The Board solemnly considered the matter for some time, and in 1825 contracted with Cottle's Ship Yard in north Salem, Massachusetts, to build a forty-ton schooner. This tiny vessel, forty-nine feet long, thirteen feet wide, and six feet deep, was not only small but ill-constructed and unseaworthy. She was supposed to be ready to sail in November 1825, but delays prevented her completion until January of the following year. This necessitated her sailing through high southern latitudes under stormy winter conditions. Nevertheless, the Board, naming her the *Missionary Packet,* obtained the services of James Hunnewell to take her to the islands. She sailed on January 18, 1826, with the reverend gentlemen of the Board wishing the captain and crew Godspeed. The editor of Hunnewell's journal remarked, "Seldom have those who go down to the sea in ships needed it more."[4]

Hunnewell was a remarkable man. He did not come from a seafaring family, but so strong was his desire to go to sea that his mother allowed him to do so at the age of fourteen.

Before the War of 1812 he made a long voyage on the brig *Fairy* which took him to the Mediterranean and many of the ports of Europe. He was land-bound during the war, but in 1815 at the age of twenty-one made a voyage to China and after its completion, left Boston again in October 1816 under Captain Blanchard in the brig *Bordeaux Packet* for a voyage to California and the Hawaiian Islands. The brig was sold and paid for in sandalwood. To Hunnewell was left the job of collecting it. This he did, and in 1818 he embarked on the ship *Osprey* for China where he disposed of his wood; he returned on the ship *Ida* the next year. Back in Boston, he and Susanna Lamson were married on December 23, and he left as mate on the *Thaddeus* bound for the Sandwich Islands with the first company of missionaries. On this voyage James Hunnewell formed a lasting friendship with the missionaries and a lasting interest in the work of the American Board.

The desire to establish a trading business in the Hawaiian Islands prompted him to offer to take the *Missionary Packet* (nicknamed in the islands the *Ten Commandments*) out to Hawaii at no charge, provided the Board would pay and feed the crew and allow him to carry forty or fifty barrels in her bulk cargo. When he saw the craft ready to sail with only one foot of freeboard after she was loaded, he began to have serious misgivings. His crew consisted of two Hawaiians who were reliable and two Americans who were not. In the first rough weather, four days after sailing, the low freeboard became a problem. Hunnewell wrote in his journal, "A man at the pump was like being on a half-tide rock, always wet."[5] One at the helm was often wet up to his hips. During heavy weather leaks required four hundred strokes per hour at the pumps. The water ran not only through her decks and around

31. Schooner *Missionary Packet*

the deck trunk, but also in at the stern and around the rudder case. A steady stream of water came over the cabin floor from aft running forward. Another large leak, which was stopped, developed between the pumps. The decks were often full of water and the vessel pitched heavily. Hunnewell put into Rio for much-needed repairs and caulking, and the two American sailors refused to go further. After leaving Rio a man fell overboard but was rescued by the remaining sailor in a boat, leaving Hunnewell alone on the *Missionary Packet* for a short time. After stopping at the Falklands he fought his way through the Straits of Magellan and came into the Pacific on August 22. For the rest of the voyage he had calmer weather and he arrived at Lahaina Roads on October 20, 1826, and in

Honolulu on the following day after a long passage of two hundred seventy-six days. In fact, Hunnewell considered it the longest on record. He turned the *Packet* over to Levi Chamberlain, business agent for the American Board, and, with the forty barrels of merchandise which he had carried out, set himself up in business. The mission used the *Missionary Packet* for supplying their posts and chartering to the merchants, but she was a white elephant and in 1836 they sold her to a ship carpenter who renamed her *Honolulu.* After being rebuilt, she was taken over by French Catholic missionaries. She was wrecked on one of her cruises around Micronesia.

Twenty years later Christianity was fairly established throughout the Hawaiian Islands and the Hawaiian Christians began to think of sending missionaries to the many islands of Micronesia to the west. They formed the Hawaiian Mission Society and the American Board decided to cooperate in their undertaking. In 1850 the schooner *Caroline* was chartered to carry three missionaries and their wives and two Hawaiian assistants to Micronesia, but lack of money prevented running her regularly. In 1853 they launched an appeal to send a mission to the Marquesans where English missionaries had failed.

At this time Titus Cohen, a veteran in the missionary movement attached to the Church in Hilo, proposed that, since small contributions from English children had built the mission ships *John Wesley* and *John Williams,* why could not American children build a similar vessel and finance it by selling ten-cent shares. The American Board thought this was a splendid idea and put his proposal into effect, naming their new vessel the *Morning Star.* An appeal was made all over the country in 1856, and the response was swift. (Some of the contributions were practical rather than financial, for a Boston Sunday School sent a chronometer and the children of a mission in Constantinople donated a speaking trumpet.) The vessel was oversubscribed with enough money remaining to maintain her. She was built in three months at Chelsea, Massachusetts, in the yard of Jotham Stetson and was launched on November 12, 1856, a new hermaphrodite brig of one hundred and fifty-six tons. A service was conducted the last day of November at the Park Street Church, and on December 2, under Captain Samuel G. Moore she sailed from Boston's India Wharf to the accompaniment of "Greenland's icy mountains" sung by the assembled multitude. She performed valiant service until 1866 when she was no longer seaworthy and a replacement had to be found.

With the money received from her sale, and with the children providing additional funds, another hermaphrodite brig named *Morning Star II* was built at East Boston and sailed in November 1866 under Hiram Bingham, Jr. This vessel had one hundred and fifty thousand stockholders. One of them, a small boy, wandered into the shipyard during construction and climbed aboard. When the foreman told him not to touch anything and to be careful, he replied, "It's all right, I am one of the owners." She carried on the work in the Gilbert Islands, to Ponape, Kusaie, and other points in Micronesia until she ran on a reef in late 1869.

The second was followed by a third *Morning Star* built at East Boston by the same firm. She arrived in Honolulu under Captain Nathaniel Matthews on July 3, 1871, and started on her Micronesian rounds. In 1872, *Morning Star III* made the last visit of one of these vessels to the Marquesas Islands, where the work had been carried on under difficulties. Some of the native missionaries stayed on, but the whites were withdrawn and the endeavor to all intents and purposes was discontinued. In 1875 she was commanded by Captain Andrew D. Colcord, member of a well-known seafaring family, and in 1878 Captain Isaiah Bray took her over. When Bray returned to Honolulu in 1881 he wrote, "We have sailed fifteen thousand seven hundred and eight-three miles and carried two hundred and forty-three passengers."[6] In 1884 under Captain Garland, *Morning Star III* was thrown broadside to on a reef near Kusaie, only about five miles from where her predecessor had gone ashore. The passengers and cargo were removed but the vessel was a complete wreck.

It was decided that the next vessel should have steam power, and in December 1883 the contract was made with the New England Shipbuilding Company of Bath, Maine, for *Morning Star IV*. She slid into the Kennebec River on August 6, 1884. Far larger than her predecessors, she was four hundred and seventy-one tons, a hundred and thirty feet long, thirty feet beam, and twelve feet deep. Of barkentine rig with a mainmast of iron that doubled as a smokestack, she was powered by a hundred-and-fifty-horsepower compound engine, calculated to give her a speed of about seven knots. Her figurehead was of a life-sized woman wearing a simple crown and pointing with her index finger of the right hand at an open Bible held in the palm of her left. According to Captain Garland, the Bible was arranged so that it could be removed in bad weather. Shares in this vessel cost twenty-five cents. She left Boston in 1884 under Captain Isaiah Bray with George F. Garland as first mate. Steam power was used for the first time in the Straits of Magellan. As she came into Punta Arenas anchorage under bare poles, the harbormaster hailed her and asked, "What are you Captain, the phantom ship?"[7] She arrived in Honolulu in mid-March 1885, and about six weeks later

32. *Morning Star I*

33. *Morning Star II*

34. *Morning Star IV*

35. *Morning Star VI*

started on her Micronesian rounds. Captain Bray was succeeded by H. N. Turner who, in turn, was succeeded by Captain George F. Garland, who continued with her and her successor *Morning Star V* for over twenty years.

During the time of *Morning Star IV* missionary work in Micronesia ran into difficulties. In 1887, Spain took over the Caroline Islands and Germany the Marshalls, and in 1892

NEW ENGLAND AND THE SOUTH SEAS

Great Britain annexed the Gilberts. The Spaniards forbade the *Star* and the missionaries to visit certain islands and destroyed a great deal of mission property. But in 1889, after the Spanish American War, when the islands were sold to Germany, the work was continued with some restrictions. The *Morning Star IV* was a good vessel and served her purpose well until 1900 when she was sold into the merchant service on the West coast to avoid the expense of major repairs. The Hawaiian Board now closed out its interest in the Micronesian mission work, leaving the American Board of Commissioners to continue alone. The Board purchased from the Maine Seacoast Mission the four-year-old steamer *Sunbeam* of four hundred and three tons. She was one hundred and thirty feet long, thirty feet wide, and nine and five-tenths feet deep, with a speed of some ten or eleven knots. Her name was changed to *Morning Star V,* and seafaring men considered her entirely unsuitable for the missionaries' purposes.[8] Shares to raise the $37,000 necessary to buy, repair, and adapt her for Pacific work were sold again at ten cents. She left Boston, June 11, 1904 and the Reverend Hiram Bingham, Jr., who had been out on both *Morning Star I* and *II* offered the prayer at her dedication. She did not go the usual way round the Horn or through the Straits of Magellan, but crossed the Atlantic to the Mediterranean and through the Suez Canal to reach Ponape on October 27. The opinion of nautical men was correct for she was a poor sea boat and far too expensive to run. Besides, in the meantime, regular steamship service had been established with the Gilberts and Marshalls. The Board put her up for sale late in 1905, but there were no buyers until three years later. This was the end of the *Morning Star* series. But there is a sequel.

During World War II, when a small group of American

soldiers landed on a Micronesian island and proceeded up the beach preparing to meet resistance, natives came out of the bushes and the leader advancing with outstretched hands said, "Good morning, we are Christians from Boston." There were many instances of this kind, and Senator Mead of New York said on the floor of Congress that, "American doughboys are reaping heavily where missionaries have so long and patiently sown."[9]

When the Japanese overran the islands most of the American Board missionaries escaped but their work had been done with surprising thoroughness. After the war when a United States Naval Commission was sent to each island to find out what the people wanted first and needed most, they were amazed to be told most frequently, "Send back the missionaries."[10] The Navy sent a special representative to the American Board in Boston asking them to resume work in the Marshalls and Carolines, and the Reverend Eleanor Wilson went out from Honolulu on a navy landing craft. Again the Board turned to the state of Maine and at East Boothbay purchased the schooner *Norseman,* sixty-three and a half feet over-all, with a diesel engine, a two-way radio, and proper long-range navigating equipment. As in earlier days, a farewell service was held for the new *Morning Star VI* at Lewis Wharf in Boston, Sunday, July 27, 1947, at which a message was received from ex-Senator Hiram Bingham, grandson of the first missionary to the Hawaiian Islands and son of the captain of the *Morning Star II.* She sailed, under Captain Price Lewis, with two thousand Bibles on board and a crew of college students. Going by way of the Panama Canal, she arrived in Honolulu on December 6, 1947, to an enthusiastic welcome. On Washington's Birthday 1948, manned by a crew of natives, she was delivered to the Reverend Eleanor Wilson at Kusaie.

NEW ENGLAND AND THE SOUTH SEAS

Eleanor Wilson was another New Englander from Connecticut who grew up in Cambridge, Massachusetts, and had long been associated with the Board as a missionary. She learned navigation and sailed *Morning Star VI* for thousands of miles throughout the Caroline and Marshall islands. While she was home on leave in 1951 the missionary schooner, badly in need of repairs, while being towed from Ponape to the Marshalls, was battered by a storm and lost. Another *Morning Star* has not replaced her but the work of the Mission still goes on, work that has been continuous ever since the *Thaddeus,* with Hiram Bingham's first little group, landed in the Hawaiian Islands in 1819.

The eighteenth century delighted in the accounts of the free and easy life of the South Sea Islanders in the published voyages of the explorers. The Polynesian was the perfect "natural man" to those who followed the beguiling philosophy of Rousseau. The Polynesian was something less than that to the Fundamentalists of the nineteenth century. No one had any right to have that much fun! Hence, when the idea of foreign missions stimulated the enthusiasm of the devout the length and breadth of New England, what region should more appropriately receive first attention than the South Seas. In this they were following the lead of the London Missionary Society; besides, there were altogether too many accounts of the delight Yankee sailors took in the pleasure of a stay at any one of a hundred islands, while their wives stayed home and went to church! A scrimshawed whale's tooth graphically sharpens this dichotomy of the sailor's life. On one side is a stylish New England lady in a hoop skirt; on the other, a sultry South Sea maiden under a palm tree. Around them the sailor's sentiment reads: "To our wives and sweethearts. May they never meet." A good reason why the American Board decided to send only married missionaries accompanied by their wives!

I suppose the long-range goal of the American Board was the eventual conversion of all of the heathens of the world. The immediate goals, however, were more modest. Many of the places selected as starting points were especially difficult but there was no lack of volunteer toilers in the Lord's vineyards. Adoniram Judson took a group to India and ended up spending much of his life among the Karin tribes of the Burmese hills. Asher Wright picked the proud New York State Iroquois, and Hiram Bingham and his associates were sent to the lewd and lascivious Hawaiians. As it turned out, this was the most successful mission of them all. So successful was it in fact that up to about 1840 it had the advantage of a state religion. Afterward government policy became religiously tolerant and Catholics, Mormons, and Episcopalians arrived and were later joined by other Christian sects and by Buddhists. New England Congregationalism, however, set a stamp upon the Islands that, in spite of all later accretions, is unmistakable. The missionaries largely accomplished what they set out to do in the Hawaiian Islands, and the extension of the mission work from there throughout Micronesia was attended with notable success that has survived to a considerable extent changes of colonial governments and the devastation of war.

Although with the descendants of some of the early traders, missionaries' sons went into business, agriculture, finance, or industry, and established dynasties of solid citizens who controlled the economy of the islands for many years. It is little wonder that they did so. The mission men and women who came and stayed, while they may not have had the difficulties encountered by their colleagues in other lands, did not have an easy time. It required a tenaciousness, patience, native intelligence, faith, and optimism not always combined in an individual. Those who did not have it returned to the United States. Those who did passed these attributes on to their children and fortified them with a good education, usually at Yale. Today there is still a strong New England, New Haven-oriented, slant to the upper economic brackets of Hawaiian society. A Yankee feels at home there.

VI ~

YANKEES IN ISLAND POLITICS

The entry of New Englanders into island politics added a new aspect to their impact on the area, one with varying degrees of influence. North and south across the central Pacific, and from Hawaii in the east to the Bonin Islands in the west, Americans tried their hands at governing. Occasionally accidental, occasionally premeditated, sometimes as colonial ventures, sometimes as advisors to island kings, they made their influence felt. Where they infiltrated, forced themselves, or were invited depended upon circumstances of time and place. Often they vanished as suddenly as they appeared, occasionally they stayed for long periods, and in some cases their successors are still on the job.

After the first contact of traders with the Hawaiian Islands, sentiment in native governmental circles inclined toward the British. It was even stronger after 1789 when John Young, the kidnaped mate of the *Eleanora,* and Isaac Davis, the sole survivor of the *Fair American* massacre, became the principal advisers to King Kamehameha I. Although they had served on American vessels, both were English. Neither was well educated but they were men of great common sense; furthermore they knew how to handle cannon. The king made them chiefs and they married into high native society. (Young's granddaughter, Emma, later became queen.) Young and Davis served the king well, as advisers and artillerymen, during his conquest of the islands and in suppressing the revolts of other chiefs. In 1795 Kamehameha had sixteen white men in his service who manned his cannon in the conquest of Oahu which gave him authority over all of the islands excepting Kauai and Niihau. These islands came under his domain in 1810 when the chief of Kauai, Kaumualii, visited Kamehameha under the protection of Captain Jonathan Winship and acknowledged him as king. On this occasion some of the king's advisers recommended poisoning Kaumualii. Davis warned the Kauai chief of the plot, and, as a result lost his own life, for he was poisoned by the conspirators.

Kamehameha's British leanings received their greatest encouragement in January 1794 when Captain George Vancouver, in H.M.S. *Discovery,* returning to the Hawaiian Islands from his explorations on the Northwest Coast, arrived at Hilo where the king was living. Vancouver sailed to Kealakekua Bay, with Kamehameha on board, and spent six weeks entertaining His Majesty. The ship's carpenters built for the king the thirty-six-foot *Britannia,* the first vessel ever constructed in the islands. Vancouver gave the Hawaiian monarch much sound advice on governing his kingdom, relations with foreigners, and the management of armed forces. Kamehameha was so impressed that on February 21 a grand council of chiefs was held on board the *Discovery* and Hawaii was formally placed under the protection of Great Britain. As the British flag was raised over the islands, the natives shouted,

YANKEES IN ISLAND POLITICS

"We are men of Britain," and the salute was fired. Vancouver's additions to the British domain were never ratified by the government in London and the opportunity was missed to add another colonial star to the imperial crown.

During the first quarter of the nineteenth century the early enthusiasm of the Hawaiian chiefs for the British was gradually offset by the multiplicity of American contacts. The increasing number of American vessels visiting the islands and the vigor of the Yankee fur and sandalwood traders began to make itself felt. This influence was augmented by the arrival of the first American whaler in 1819, and more beneficially increased by the arrival of the first missionaries the same year.

There is no doubt that the missionaries above all others had the best interests of the natives at heart. Unlike their contemporaries, the whalers and sandalwood traders who exploited the natives and resources of the islands for their own benefits, the missionaries genuinely wanted not only to Christianize the Hawaiians but also to civilize them, to educate them, and to raise their economy to a higher standard. These good and serious men and women worked hard at it and the fun-loving Polynesians, while they were not wholly convinced of the good that might accrue to them through hard work, devotion, and high morals, realized that the missionaries were acting in their behalf and respected them for it. Young and Davis were also instrumental in helping the missionaries off to a good start. When the first group requested permission to land on the Islands, Kamehameha asked his English advisers whether or not the men of God should be allowed to do so. They answered affirmatively, saying, "These men from abroad bring the faith which has made England and America great." The King then consented to let them land. Gradually the missionaries gained the confidence of the chiefs who sought their advice and counsel on many matters. Two men, the Reverend William Richards and the physician Gerritt Pamele Judd, resigned from the mission and became high officials and important men in the Hawaiian kingdom.

The stature and influence of the Reverend William Richards in Hawaii dates from 1824 when his advice helped Hoapili, the Christian governor of Maui, to suppress a revolt on the island of Kauai. Richards told Hoapili that the enemy was clearly at fault and that his were the forces of right to whom a just God would give victory, especially if the governor strictly observed the Sabbath during his campaign. Hoapili

36. Honolulu and Diamond Head

followed the advice, Richard's predictions came true, and the rebellion was smashed. The following year the redoubtable Richards added to his stature by taking a firm stand against the crew of the London whale ship *Daniel* which arrived at Lahaina on October 3, 1825. On this occasion the whalers found that the new native law against vice which was in effect forbade Hawaiian women to go aboard ships. Several of the crew threatened Richards and his wife with death if he did not have the law repealed, and four days later only the interference of the natives saved the missionary's life when a large number

YANKEES IN ISLAND POLITICS

of sailors entered his yard armed with knives and pistols. Hoapili then came to his assistance and placed a guard around his home until the *Daniel* took her departure.

In January 1826, Lt. John "Mad Jack" Percival, a native of Sandwich on Cape Cod, arrived in Honolulu with the U.S.S. *Dolphin*. He disgraced himself and his country by forcing repeal of the vice law in that port by threatening to fire on the Hawaiians. When the repeal was announced in Honolulu, "a shout of triumph ran through the shipping."[1] The *Dolphin* remained in port for two months longer and during this time the vice law remained suspended and women went freely aboard the ships. But, at Lahaina, Rev. Richards stood firm, although luckily he was absent when the crews of several whale ships landed there in October 1826 and threatened to massacre him and his whole family. The natives prevented the rioters from demolishing his house and the native women fled to the mountains, while the sailors destroyed and plundered native houses and then sailed off for Oahu.

The United States Navy entered the picture a second time the same month as the outrage was going on at Lahaina, with the arrival of Captain Thomas Ap Catesby Jones in the U.S.S. *Peacock* which had been sent to secure debts due to American citizens by the Hawaiian government. During three months' stay in the Islands he collected thirty or more American runaway sailors, and then entered into negotiations with the king and chiefs regarding the claims of American traders. Captain Jones reduced many of these exorbitant claims, yet they still ran to around half a million dollars. To pay them an edict was issued that every man should deliver half a picul of sandalwood or pay four Spanish dollars, and that every woman should deliver a twelve-by-six-foot mat or pay one dollar before September 1, 1827—all proceeds to be applied against the payment of claims. At a council held in late December called by the queen regent, the terms of the first commerical treaty between the Hawaiian government and a foreign power was concluded with the United States over the objections of Mr. Richard Charlton, the British Minister, who claimed that the islanders were subjects of Great Britain and had no right to make treaties with other powers.

The third and last of Richards' yearly troubles at Lahaina came in October 1827 with the arrival of the English whaler *John Palmer,* commanded by an American. Several native girls were taken on board and Hoapili, hearing of it, demanded that they be returned on shore. The captain ignored the demand, but, while he was ashore, Hoapili seized him and demanded that the women be released. Captain Clarke promised the women would be returned the next morning and was allowed to return aboard his ship. In the meantime, the crew opened fire on the village with a nine-pound gun and aimed five ineffective shots at Richard's house. Clarke sailed for Honolulu the next morning without releasing the women. The three episodes at Lahaina created such a stir in Honolulu that even some of the native chiefs began joining the captains in condemning the minister, who was requested to attend a council meeting in Honolulu and answer various charges. Two meetings were held, and Richards acquitted himself so well that the chiefs decided that there was no question of the truth of his position. More guns were placed on the fort at Lahaina, and the guard for his protection was strengthened. Shortly thereafter the first written laws against murder, theft, adultery, rum-selling, and gambling were published. No outrages occurred thereafter.

The missionary influence on the king and chiefs was unofficial until 1836 when Richards accepted the position of adviser, chaplain, and instructor in the science of government to the king and chiefs, and resigned his connection with the American Mission. Thereafter until his death, November 7, 1847, he was constantly in the public service. From July 8, 1842 until March 23, 1845 he served as Ambassador for the Hawaiian government in Europe and the United States, and on April 13, 1846 he was made Minister of Public Instruction, a post which he held until his death. It was he who was responsible, the year after his appointment, for the Hawaiian code of laws and Bill of Rights. In 1840 he wrote Hawaii's first constitution, providing for an elaborate legislative, judicial, and administrative system. He was instrumental during his ambassadorship in obtaining guarantees of the independence of Hawaii by Britain, France, and the United States. On his death another missionary, Richard Armstrong, succeeded him as Minister of Public Instruction.

Dr. Gerritt Pamele Judd was only twenty-four years old when he and his young wife sailed with the third company of missionaries on the ship *Parthian* from Boston in the autumn of 1827. During the usual rough passage the young doctor showed his forcefulness of character by taking the lead in getting necessities and small comforts from an unusually obtuse curmudgeon of a captain. They arrived in Honolulu in late March 1828 and were put up for a time by the Hiram Binghams.

The first morning there, as Mrs. Bingham was not well, Mrs. Judd got up early to get breakfast. But, said she, on going into the kitchen: "judge of my dismay . . . to find a tall native man, clad much in the style of John the Baptist in the wilderness, seated before the fire, frying taro. . . . I stood aghast, in doubt whether to retire, or stand my ground like a brave woman, and was ready to cry with annoyance and vexation. . . .

I am verdant enough to be shocked, and shall use all my influence to increase the sale and use of American cottons."2 It took a little time for Yankees of the pious variety to get used to nonchalant Polynesian ways.

Dr. Judd began his medical duties at once, and year after year put in long hours riding over mountain trails, passing from island to island in schooners and native canoes, administering to the sick, helping with the delivery of babies, and making brilliant observations on the local diseases. In September 1840 he guided Lt. Charles Wilkes and members of his exploring expedition to the active lava pit of Kilauea. Judd nearly lost his life here in an attempt to collect liquid lava in a frying pan. An explosion was followed by a fiery jet burst, and a river of fire rolled toward him. Trying to escape the intense heat, he could not climb the projecting wall until a native guide reached down, seized his hand and pulled him to safety. The crater filled up in a few minutes and overflowed.

When the Reverend William Richards went off to America and Europe to negotiate for formal recognition of Hawaiian independence, Kamehameha III persuaded Dr. Judd to fill Richards' place during his absence. Like Richards, Judd found it impossible to be a missionary and an adviser of the government simultaneously, so he resigned from the mission on April 19, 1842, although he agreed to continue to care for its members' medical needs. Besides Richards' duties, Judd was made head of the Treasury Board of the Kingdom and was empowered to receive all taxes, duties, land rents, "and every kind of property which can be made use of in paying government debts."3

Judd had a long statesmanlike and interesting career as the confidante of the Hawaiian king. One of his triumphs occurred when Lord George Paulet arrived on February 10,

1843 in H.M.S. *Carysfort* and made pre-emptory demands for the surrender of the Hawaiian kingdom to Great Britain. Richards was on his way to Britain to negotiate on this very aspect of international relations, so on the forty-year-old Judd fell the responsibility of maintaining Hawaiian independence and preventing bloodshed. He counseled the king to cede the islands, but under protest that Paulet was not the rightful representative of his government. On February 25, 1843, the Hawaiian flag came down and the British flag went up. Judd was retained as the King's Deputy, but he smuggled the government archives and treasury records into the tomb of Hawaii's kings and did his work there at night, using the coffin of Queen Kaahumanu as a desk. The protest to Queen Victoria which he prepared was signed by Kamehameha III and arrived at the British Foreign Office at the same time as Lord George's report on the taking over of the islands. Paulet's superior, Rear Admiral Richard Thomas, was sent from Valparaiso, reaching Honolulu on July 30, 1843. He restored Hawaii's freedom at a brilliant ceremony that returned the island to Kamehameha III as an independent sovereign. Following the ceremony the first salute to the Hawaiian flag was fired from the guns of the *Carysfort,* H.M.S. *Dublin* and the U.S. frigate *Constellation.* In 1848 Judd was instrumental in the formation of a stock company which attempted to take over vast tracts of public lands on a hundred-year lease, resulting in the great Mahele Division of the kingdom, traditionally the king's sole property. For the first time a Hawaiian owned his real estate and could sell or mortgage it as he wished. Of the many years of devoted service to his adopted country Judd wrote, "God has heard my prayer. He has prospered my efforts and permitted me to witness the Hawaiian government independent and free."[4]

NEW ENGLAND AND THE SOUTH SEAS

The missionaries and their sons were not only a force in the development of the government structure of the islands, they also played no small part in the development of its growing economy. The Dole Company, principal pineapple grower in the islands, is a missionary name. Two of the five great sugar companies—Castle and Cooke, and Alexander and Baldwin—bear the names of four missionary families. F. P. Alexander and H. P. Baldwin, sons of missionaries, carried out the great irrigation project on Mauai which brought water from the very wet side of the island to the dry side and made the rich land there usable.

Yankee traders were equally effective in business. Typical was the young Bostonian James Hunnewell, who, in 1826, had brought the American Board's little schooner *Missionary Packet,* loaded in part with his own trade goods, to Hawaii. Shortly thereafter he set himself up in business on an excellent piece of property in what is now the center of Honolulu. Purchasing sandalwood from the natives and furs and skins from ships which arrived from the American coast, he transshipped them to the Chinese market and built a substantial business. He also sent consignments of goods to California and South American ports, and he bought and sold anything where a profit could be made, from Yankee notions to ships' stores. He also acted as an agent for the thriving Boston firm of Bryant and Sturgis. As he prospered he became a man of influence in the islands.

That Hunnewell was not only an astute businessman but also a perceptive judge of character and ability is demonstrated by his hiring of another Charlestown man as his clerk and assistant in November 1828. Henry A. Peirce, then twenty-one, sailed to the Northwest Coast as a crew member of the brig *Griffon* (commanded by his brother Marcus and owned by Bryant and Sturgis). In the course of the voyage he rose from sailor to supercargo and took over the West Coast fur trading with the Indians. The *Griffon* carried in her cargo a consignment of blue cloth to James Hunnewell, and when the vessel reached Honolulu young Peirce left her for shore employment with his fellow townsman. In 1830, Hunnewell, whose assets had risen from $5,000 to $67,000, turned the business over to Peirce, now his partner, and, leaving him $20,000 with which to conduct it, returned to Boston on the brig *Owhyhee*. He settled in Charlestown and was active in shipping business circles around Boston for many years, but he continued his interest in Hawaii and supported educational and charitable activities there. On his death in 1869, King Kamehameha V wrote to his son, James F. Hunnewell:

The name of the late James Hunnewell was early associated with the commercial interest of these islands, and his long and useful life was marked by such constant good will to my kingdom that I shall always cherish his memory with sincere regard. Although he was only removed in the fulness of time, I deeply sympathize with you in the loss of such a parent, but I congratulate you in the inheritance of such an honored name.[5]

Peirce was energetic and sensible and the business prospered under his management. In 1832 he erected a new stone building to replace the thatch-and-mud houses formerly occupied by the company. At the end of the following year the partnership of Hunnewell and Peirce ended, and the senior partner withdrew; Peirce took on a new partner in Thomas D. Hinckley, another Bostonian, and the firm became Peirce and Hinckley. This new partnership, which lasted less than a year, was dissolved at the end of September 1834.

(Hinckley's health had deteriorated, and he wrote Hunnewell that he could no longer carry on business as an equal partner. He sailed for Boston later in the year, but died at sea during the voyage home.)

The few months of having a partner, however, gave Peirce an opportunity to leave Honolulu. Chartering the Salem-built brig *Becket,* then owned by Kamehameha III, with Captain Charles Brewer as master and himself as supercargo, Peirce set sail for China and Kamchatka with a cargo of sandalwood and pearl shell. The association of Pierce and Brewer was a fortuitous circumstance, for it began a close relationship of two able men that continued for some years. Peirce disposed of the *Becket's* cargo successfully at Lintin Island, Hongkong, and purchased merchandise suitable for trade in the Hawaiian Islands and with the Russian settlement at Kamchatka. Arriving at the harbor of Petropavlovsk in early June, he sold part of his China goods, and he and Brewer celebrated by giving a Fourth of July party on board the *Becket.*

Peirce's attempt to open trade with Russia, which seemed successful on this voyage, received a setback the following year when he sent Captain Brewer in the ship *Rasselas,* formerly a Boston–Liverpool packet, on a voyage to China and the Siberian settlements. The profit of this voyage was so small that the new trade route was not pursued. Peirce continued to operate the business alone after the retirement of Hinckley. He successfully collected a cargo of sandalwood for J. P. Sturgis of Canton, even though that commodity was now becoming exceedingly rare in the Islands, and he made a successful voyage to Mexico to collect specie belonging to Sturgis to pay for the wood. In February 1836 he decided to take Captain Charles Brewer into partnership with him, and the business continued under their names.

YANKEES IN ISLAND POLITICS

Brewer was also from Boston, where he had been born on March 27, 1804. He had followed the sea since he was seventeen years old, shipping first as a sailor before the mast, and had made voyages to Calcutta and Europe. An avid reader of Cook's voyages when he was a boy, he was inspired to ship on a voyage which would touch at the Hawaiian Islands, so he signed aboard the *Paragon* to collect sandalwood. Brewer made his second voyage to the Hawaiian Islands as first mate of the brig *Chinchilla* under the Marbleheader Captain Thomas Meek. Within twenty-four days of when James Hunnewell left Boston for his precarious voyage in the *Missionary Packet,* Brewer left New York on the *Chinchilla,* both bound for Honolulu, neither with any knowledge of the other's plans. Brewer continued with Captain Meek, and made three voyages in the *Chinchilla* to Honolulu, China, Kamchatka, and Alaska over a three-year period. The two men became very close friends. After a visit home which lasted several months, he returned to the same trade in the brig *Ivanhoe* of Boston under Captain Snow, a difficult man with a violent temper. On one occasion in Honolulu, Brewer was ordered to throw overboard some plants which the supercargo had picked up on the coast of Mexico. Reluctant to do this, he took one of the plants ashore where it flourished; thus the beautiful night-blooming cereus was introduced to the Islands. He left Captain Snow in Honolulu and made voyages for furs to the Northwest Coast and trading trips along the coast of Mexico and the Gulf of California for hides and horses. While trading further with the Russian settlements around Kamchatka, he discovered a new and prolific whaling ground in the Ochotsk Sea, which gave a new lease on life to the whaling industry out of Honolulu. It was at this point that Brewer made the voyage on the *Becket* with Henry A. Peirce.

NEW ENGLAND AND THE SOUTH SEAS

After the establishment of the partnership of Peirce and Brewer, Peirce took the opportunity to visit home again but returned to Hawaii in 1837. The energetic Brewer now became the more active partner, but for several years the two men took turns visiting their homes in Boston and conducting business in Honolulu. In 1838 Peirce married Miss Susan R. Thompson of Charlestown and established a home in Boston. On the side he, Hunnewell, and Brewer operated various vessels in trade between Boston, Tahiti, Honolulu, and the Californian and Mexican coasts. In 1840 it was Brewer's turn to come home, where he also married. In 1843 Peirce retired and the firm became C. Brewer and Company. Peirce was an active man, however, and he did not swallow the anchor for long. He went into other ventures, sometimes alone, sometimes with his old partner Hunnewell, and for a while took an interest in Russell and Company at Canton. By 1855 he was settled in New England as Consul for Hawaii at the ports of Portsmouth, Portland, and Boston, an office which he held for some years. In 1869 he returned to the Pacific as Minister Resident to the Hawaiian Islands, appointed by the State Department, and it was probably at his suggestion that the United States Government invited King Kalakaua to visit the United States. He accompanied the king and a large reception was held for Kalakaua in Boston where he was lavishly entertained by James Hunnewell and Charles Brewer. Peirce resigned his ministership in 1877, returning from Honolulu by way of San Francisco and across the continent by rail to Boston, where he lived until his death in 1884.

During 1845 Captain Brewer decided to relinquish his control of the firm and sold a one-third interest to each of two other Bostonians, J. F. B. Marshall and Francis Johnson. That same year his nephew, Charles Brewer, II, with his wife sailed from Boston to the Hawaiian Islands on the Salem ship *Mindoro*. Johnson withdrew after a couple of years because of ill-health and returned to Boston where he died in 1848. Marshall continued actively in the business as did Charles Brewer, II, and so the Boston management of this firm continued, although its affairs became more involved and at one point it was nearly liquidated. Captain Brewer himself retired from the business but operated a shipping firm in Boston with his old friends Hunnewell and Peirce until shortly before the Civil War. He then continued on his own under the name of Charles Brewer and Company. He retired in 1884 and died the following year. In writing his reminiscences at the age of eighty he said, "I can look back and realize that the desires and ambitions of my youth have been fully gratified, for it has certainly been my good fortune to visit almost every part of the globe. My life at the Sandwich Islands, during a period of nearly twenty-six years, was a very pleasant one, and I shall always remember with gratitude the kindness I received from the many friends in Honolulu, and especially from His Majesty, King Kamehameha III., who from his boyhood to his death was always my firm friend."[6]

It is not necessary to follow further the affairs of the powerful firm of C. Brewer and Company, Ltd., under Charles Brewer, II, and others. Business changed from outfitting whaling ships at the port of Honolulu to transporting merchandise for the California Gold Rush, but the able Yankees from Massachusetts had laid the foundations of the company solidly. Hunnewell, Peirce, Brewer, Marshall, and Brewer, II, were all cut from the same bolt of cloth, and conducted their business with shrewdness, energy, and honesty. Their transactions fanned out into sugar, insurance, steamships, and real estate, and a trickle of other Boston men continued in their offices.

NEW ENGLAND AND THE SOUTH SEAS

37. The Siva dance of Samoa

Between the activities of New England missionaries and traders, the future of the Hawaiian Islands was almost foreordained. Agitation for annexation to the United States began as early as 1853 and 1854 when United States Commissioner Luther Severance was writing about annexation to political leaders in his home state of Maine. The troubled political career of the Hawaiian monarchs, however, continued until a revolution forced Queen Liliuokalani from the throne in 1893. An appeal for annexation to the United States was rejected by President Cleveland on the ground that America's diplomatic representative aided by United States Marines had improperly backed the revolution. A republic was proclaimed on the Fourth of July 1894 with Sanford B. Dole as President. A second appeal for annexation, made to President McKinley in 1898, was successful; the islands were formally organized into the Territory of Hawaii and accepted by United States Minister Harold M. Sewall of the famous shipbuilding family of Bath, Maine. A long and tortuous

YANKEES IN ISLAND POLITICS

political evolution reached its logical conclusion when Hawaii became our fiftieth state.

Sewall had also played an important part in United States affairs with another Polynesian group in the 1880's. Samoa had been surveyed by Commodore Charles Wilkes on his exploring expedition, and in 1877 the American Consul there raised the flag, but the action was repudiated by our government in Washington. In 1848, by treaty with the natives, the United States obtained Pagopago as a coaling station. At the same time Germany and Great Britain also staked out claims to Samoa but no single power acquired the islands. In 1887 and 1888 there was a civil war over the succession of native kingship, with the Germans supporting Tamasese and the British and Americans supporting Malietoa. The Germans

38. Residence of the Samoan Chief Mataafa

deported Malietoa, but the fight was carried on by another chief named Mataafa, whose followers killed and wounded about fifty Germans. The independence and autonomy of the islands was guaranteed at the Berlin Conference of 1889.

NEW ENGLAND AND THE SOUTH SEAS

Malietoa was restored as king. Samoa now became practically a protectorate of the three great powers who appointed a chief justice and a president of Apia municipality to carry out the provisions of the treaty. This amiable arrangement lasted until the death of Malietoa in 1898, when again two rival claimants appeared. This time the Germans supported Mataafa, while the British and Americans backed a youth named Malietoa Tanu. Again there was a civil war and several British and Americans were killed. The three powers sent out a commission to Samoa to investigate and adjust the difficulties. The situation was so complicated and embarrassing that the Berlin Treaty was abrogated in 1900 and Great Britain withdrew her claim to any part of the islands in return for German concessions elsewhere in the world. The United States withdrew from all the islands west of Tutuila, but indifferent Congresses did not act on the matter until 1926 when accession to the United States was formally approved and the administration of eastern Samoa placed in the hands of the

39. Mataafa

40. Malietoa

YANKEES IN ISLAND POLITICS

Navy Department. In 1914 a New Zealand Expeditionary Force occupied western Samoa. A New Zealand protectorate until 1962, on New Year's Day of that year western Samoa was granted complete independence.

Since the close of the Second World War, the United States has governed, as a Trust Territory under the United Nations, the Marshalls, Carolines, and Marianas (except Guam, an American territory since the Spanish-American War)—in short, all of the islands from Hawaii to Indonesia north of the equator, with the exception of the Gilberts. These islands, although they have been successively under Spanish, German, and Japanese control, still show signs of the influence of the nineteenth-century American whalers, traders, and missionaries. That this activity stretched completely across the Pacific to the very doorstep of Japan is illustrated by the experience of a New Englander in the Bonin Islands to the northwest of the Marianas.

The uninhabited Bonin Islands were discovered in 1823 by Captain James Coffin of the whaleship *Transit*. The largest of the group, Peel Island, was discovered in 1827 by Captain Frederick W. Beechey in H.M.S. *Blossom,* who found there two English whalemen, shipwrecked eight months before. Beechey surveyed Port Lloyd on Chichi-jima, and took possession of the group on behalf of King George.

Nathaniel Savory was born in Bradford, Massachusetts, July 31, 1794, and at the age of twenty went to sea. One day in 1829 his ship was in Honolulu Harbor and, while firing a salute, Savory accidentally lost a finger. He was left on shore for surgical treatment and his vessel departed. At just this time whalers returning from the Japan ground were bringing stories of the uninhabited Bonin Islands to the Hawaiian Islands. There were safe anchorages, a good climate, fertile soil, and plenty of fish and turtles in the surrounding waters. It was a perfect place for whalers to refresh but no one lived there. Here was an opportunity to establish a trading colony not to be overlooked. When Richard Charlton, British Consul in Honolulu, concocted a scheme to establish a colony on the Bonins, Nathaniel Savory entered into it with unbounded enthusiasm. A schooner was fitted out with necessities for establishing a colony and five white men were recruited. They were a diverse group. Besides Savory there were Aldin Chapin a fellow Yankee, Charles Johnson a Dane, John Millinchamp an Englishman, and Matteo Mazarro by birth an Italian but a British subject. In the spring of 1830, Charlton appointed Mazarro Governor and they set sail accompanied by twenty-five native Hawaiian men and women. They reached the Bonins on June 26, 1830, and established their settlement under the British flag. The little group prospered and Savory became a dominating influence. When Mazarro died in 1848, Savory succeeded him as governor. Two years later he married Mazarro's widow who bore him ten children. Since no power had claimed the Bonins, Savory accepted the governorship with the reservation that he owed no allegiance to Great Britain and it was his constant hope that the United States would eventually claim the islands. "Old Nat," as he was called, was a hard worker and prospered. He recovered from a setback in 1849 when two captains raided the island and carried away thousands of dollars worth of livestock and provisions and stole two thousand dollars which he had saved in twenty years of trading. He was the dominating factor in developing a rich agricultural community, raising tobacco, sugar cane, vegetables, and livestock. He made rum from sugar cane, cured tobacco, and smoked ham and bacon to sell to the visiting whale ships and his provisions were also in great demand at Guam.

YANKEES IN ISLAND POLITICS

In 1851 the first British naval visitor since Captain Beechey twenty-five years before, called at the Bonins for provisions. He was Captain Richard Collinson in H.M.S. *Enterprise* spending a winter in warm waters between two summers in the Arctic searching for Sir John Franklin. In 1853 Commodore Matthew C. Perry on his famous expedition to open the ports of Japan called at Port Lloyd in the Bonins. He purchased land for an American coaling station and drew up a code of laws for the settlers. Nathaniel Savory, who hoped that at last the islands would become a United States possession, was made chief magistrate. Perry's actions resulted in some inconclusive controversy between Great Britain and the United States regarding sovereignty but neither country was really very much interested. In 1861 the Japanese attempted to establish a colony but abandoned the project two years later. Finally in 1875 they made a second and successful attempt and two years later formally annexed the islands. Neither Britain nor the United States disputed the action. Nathaniel Savory did not see the *Miji Maru* sail into Port Lloyd for he died in 1874. His journal kept during his residence on the islands was destroyed by a tidal wave in 1872—a great historical loss. A short distance from the door of his house a tombstone reads "Sacred to the memory of Nathaniel Savory a native of Bradford, Essex County, Massachusetts, U.S.A., and one of the first settlers of this island who departed this life April 10, 1874, aged eighty years." The blood of the Essex County Savorys still flows in the Bonin Islanders but it is now well thinned by Polynesian and Japanese.

Yankee political activities followed no particular pattern. The earliest were the results of negotiations between traders and native chiefs, amounting to nothing permanent in New Zealand and Fiji, for example, to the ultimate as an integral part of the United States in Hawaii. Just as traders were forced into politics to protect their interests, so were missionaries to preserve the progress of Christianity. In the Hawaiian Islands, where the interests of traders and missionaries combined, political success was most outstanding. Missionary influence after their brief contact left not a trace in the Marquesas, but in Micronesia it was dominant until ended by world colonialism and now under the United States Trusteeship is active again. Colonialism survives in Samoa but the individual effort in the Bonins ceased long ago. Thus the political seeds were sown in diverse ways and varied are the fruits thereof.

VII ~

SEARCHING FOR PARADISE

There is something about certain villages, certain towns, certain regions and areas of the world that captures the imagination. Even after they have been seen at first hand they are more likely to be seen in the mind's eye as the pictures one has conceived from the printed page. Sometimes one wonders what the appeal can be, for it is subtle and ill-defined; at other times it is obvious—the beauty of the place, or the peculiarity of the character of its inhabitants. Perhaps it breathes a quiet serenity that enchants the visitor, or it may be that its life is turbulent, adventurous, romantic. Whatever it is, writers will descend on that region.

No region better exemplifies the continuous literary tradition than the South Seas. Ever since John Hawkesworth's account of the voyages of Byron and Wallis, and of Captain James Cook's circumnavigation in the *Endeavour* appeared in 1773,[1] hardly a year has gone by without one volume or new edition of a work on the South Seas; and the flood of letterpress seems to be rising rather than decreasing. Hundreds of books have been written on the voyages of exploration, and many have been reprinted time after time. The missionaries and their historians have contributed an equal, if less entertaining, bulk of work. Travelers of every kind have published their stories; scientists, their monographs; sailors, their adventures. The islands of the South Seas and the waters around them have been the subjects of innumerable novels and of a fantastic number of quasi-scientific and historical speculations that are almost equally fictitious. One can read almost anything about the region for it is described in every way, from paradise to hell—although the former usually prevails.

The extraordinary success and achievements of the three voyages of Captain James Cook and the publication of their results, opened a faucet which has not yet been turned off. Not until spacemen bring back records from the moon shall we see such excitement and public interest as Cook's voyages produced. And well they might, for never before had expeditions so justified their dispatch. Never before had voyages been so well planned, so well equipped, so competently carried out. Never before had there been another Cook. The history of the voyages was like a powerful three-act play with the leading character meeting a tragic death toward the end of his last voyage at the site of his greatest discovery. Competent artists and scientists sailed on each ship and their accounts and paintings enriched the official publications. Although private journals were confiscated, surreptitious accounts appeared before the Admiralty books could be published.[2]

But it was not the success of the expedition, the competence of the commander, or the publication of the handsome official volumes that caught the public imagination. It was the stories of the beauties of the islands, the salubrious climate, the fruit and other food so bountifully and easily produced, and the engaging, handsome, happy Polynesians. Here was the paradise on earth already philosophically produced in the mid-eighteenth-century European mind. Here was Rousseau's "noble savage," and Europeans took him to their hearts. Best of all, natives were sometimes brought back. Bougainville carried a Tahitian to France, and when Captain Tobias Furneaux returned in the *Adventure* from Cook's second voyage, he had on board Omai from the island of Huahine, an engaging young man who became the lion of London. Assorted natives had been exhibited in London before— Tartars from Central Asia and Eskimos brought back by Frobisher—but never before had there been one so attractive, so amiable, or one who received such publicity. Omai was wined, dined, and entertained. Poems and plays were written about him. His portrait was painted by Nathaniel Dance and by Sir Joshua Reynolds. When he was returned to his home-land on Cook's third voyage he was loaded with enough gifts, supplies, hardware, and livestock to outfit a small village.

The success of the Cook voyages led to a series of expeditions from England, France, and other countries. Besides govern-ment expeditions innumerable private commerical voyages of one kind or another were made, and many captains and sailors took pen in hand and produced books about their South Sea adventures.

Ripples from this Pacific exploration did not fail to touch the shores of America. When Cook set out on his third voyage the American Revolution was under way. Accordingly, American warships and privateers were ordered not to molest his vessels if they were encountered. Benjamin Franklin even

NEW ENGLAND AND THE SOUTH SEAS

inspired England's traditional enemies, France and Spain, to send out blanket orders to their warships to leave Cook alone.

Ledyard was the first American to write about the South Seas, but others were soon doing the same. The sealers Edmund Fanning and Benjamin Morrell from Connecticut and Amasa Delano from Massachusetts wrote best sellers. Naval officers were inspired, and Captain David Porter published an account of his cruise in the frigate *Essex* to the Pacific in 1812 to 1814 as did C. S. Stewart, chaplain of the U.S.S. *Vincennes* during its 1829–30 to the South Seas. Francis Warriner and J. N. Reynolds wrote books about the circumnavigation of the frigate *Potomac* from 1831 to 1834.

In spite of this, no real

41. Omai

piece of literature on the South Seas came out of New England for many years, although for the first half of the nineteenth century probably more New Englanders were more familiar with the islands and waters of the Pacific than any other group of men. Ralph Waldo Emerson's remark that "from 1790 to 1820, there was not a book, a speech, a conversation or a thought in the State"[3] bears repeating. But if there were no books, there were other reminders. New Englanders seemed to be bringing back native curiosities

SEARCHING FOR PARADISE

42. U.S. Frigate *Essex*

by the shipload and coral by the ton. A handsome wallpaper depicting Cook's voyages was used in houses from Augusta, Maine, to Providence, Rhode Island. When the East India Marine Society built its noble hall it employed the artist Michel Felice Cornè, then living in Salem, to paint a portrait of Captain Cook and another showing a dramatic scene of his death in Kealakekua Bay.

Richard Henry Dana was outside the South Sea literary tradition—there was no glamour in the California hide trade. No paradise could be found in the severe endless wilderness of North America, although believers in Rousseau's philosophy sought it there. Other than Polynesia, known tropical regions were disease-ridden and the philosophy itself was probably an eighteenth-century escape to the "paradise" of childhood. Coincidence had combined the paradise tradition with the South Seas and the "noble savage" with the Polynesian.

With his first book, Herman Melville introduced the truth about the South Seas into the American literary tradition. After his stay in the Typee Valley, he could not accept the paradise philosophy without reservations. But, even with his realistic approach, there was enough left to beguile the reader. Fayaway

NEW ENGLAND AND THE SOUTH SEAS

alone, sailing her canoe, was enough to stimulate the imagination. Besides, Melville was a consummate literary craftsman.

Although born in Albany, New York, in 1819, Melville was a New Englander by inheritance and by adoption. In 1841 he shipped on board the New Bedford whaler *Acushnet,* and the next four years of his life were spent wandering around the Pacific. The experiences of those four years were the basis of his most popular and best-known works.

The first book derived from his adventures, published in 1846, a year after his return, was *Typee: A Peep at Polynesian Life.* This romantic blend of fact and fiction set the tone for most subsequent writing on the South Seas. On July 9, 1842, Melville had jumped ship in the Marquesas Islands and settled down for about a month in the Typee Valley of Nuku Hiva. (In the book, Melville extended this stay to four months.) Twenty years earlier, Commodore Porter had led an expedition against the Typees and burned their villages, a circumstance which may have influenced their behavior toward Americans. Mel-

43. The *Acushnet*

SEARCHING FOR PARADISE

ville presents the Typees as more barbarous, cruel, and cannibalistic than other Marquesans—a doubtful judgment. In general, the Marquesans, reputedly the handsomest of the Polynesians, were a rather sour lot compared with the gay Tahitians or Hawaiians whom he saw later. Much ink has been spent in controversies over the autobiographical reliability of *Typee*. As a matter of fact, Melville skillfully wove together his own, sometimes elaborated, adventures, the experiences of others, and pure invention.

Melville left the Typee Valley sometime in August 1842 on the Sydney, Australia, whaler *Lucy Ann*. (In *Omoo*, this vessel became the *Julia*.) Thus he escaped from the romantic but, according to him, dangerous Marquesas to go on an unrewarding cruise. Not a single whale was taken, not a single barrel of oil added to the skimpy two hundred and fifty barrels in the *Lucy's* hold. After cruising for several weeks with little oil and a sick crew the ship

44. A native of Nuku Hiva

put in to Tahiti. Here, when the crew heard that they were not to be given an opportunity to recuperate in this favorite of watering places, they mutinied. About ten of them, including Melville, were thrown into the jail by the authorities for several weeks. Life in the "Calabooza Beretanee"—as the British jail for deserting seamen, about a mile outside of Papeete on the Broom Road was called—was, like most things in Tahiti, somewhat casual; as long as the sailors showed up to sleep there, few restrictions were placed on them during the day.

When released from his not-unpleasant incarceration, Melville teamed up with a shipmate known as Dr. Long Ghost— one of those improbable characters found in the South Seas— and the young men went to nearby Moorea, where they worked for two planters raising potatoes for the Papeete market. (One of the planters was "a tall, robust, Yankee born in the backwoods of Maine, sallow and with a long face.") The life of Melville and his companion on Moorea was apparently a happy one, largely devoted to doing as little work as possible in return for their pay. Finally they quit the planters altogether, the Maine man furnishing them with character references, and took off for an inland village where life was supposed to be less affected by European influences. There they sponged on an earnest Christian native and his family, fished in the inland lake of Temae, and enjoyed a pleasant week of uninterrupted loafing. Their idyllic existence was disturbed by the approach of strangers. Fearful of being taken as runaway sailors, they fled around the island to Papetoai Bay, a harbor of unsurpassed loveliness, where Melville spent two months. Even today Papetoai and the nearby Cook Bay look practically the same as they did when Captain Cook anchored there.* The jagged, verdant peaks tower above the deep blue water and the white surf crashes continuously on the reef outside.

Early in 1843 Melville took leave of his companion beachcomber and shipped on a whaler. After cruising for a month

---

*The remains of the stone chapel described by Melville are still standing and when I was there in 1957 we were entertained by other Yankee planters.

SEARCHING FOR PARADISE

through the Austral Islands and the equatorial whaling grounds, the ship arrived at Honolulu where he left it. When the whaler *Acushnet,* which he had deserted at Nuku Hiva, arrived for supplies and advertised him as a deserter, he decided it was time to leave. On August 4, 1843, the frigate *United States* arrived in Honolulu Harbor, and a scant fortnight later Melville shipped on board her as an ordinary seaman.

Herman Melville's cruise home provided the material for *White Jacket,* his romantic, propaganda-laden novel about the United States Navy of the period. The *United States* left Honolulu on August 20, 1843, and came to anchor in Nuku Hiva Bay on October 6, the place Melville had entered fifteen months before on the *Acushnet.* The warship then sailed for Tahiti where Melville had another week, apparently without shore leave. Leaving Matavai Bay on October 19, the frigate sailed past Moorea and laid her course for the South American coast. This was Melville's last look at a South Sea island.

Melville arrived back in Boston in October 1844 and lost no time putting his South Sea experiences into print. *Typee* was published in 1846, followed by *Omoo* in 1847, *Mardi* in 1849, *White Jacket* in 1850, and *Moby Dick* in 1851. These books—both the romanticized travelogues with their blend of fact and fiction and the novels—were the inspiration for all future American writing on the South Seas. Melville's reaction to the Polynesian islands was similar to that of most other young men before his time and since. Tahiti especially has been the subject of considerable writing of this peculiar type of fiction and fact, blended so that it is almost impossible to separate one from the other. Actually, there is hardly a book on that island of which this is not to some extent true. The eighteenth-century paradise was gone, but in its place was another paradise, based on reality but equally improbable and desirable.

As in *White Jacket,* Melville's experiences in the Pacific served him well. The background material which he accumulated on whalers, particularly the *Acushnet,* together with his

45. Sketch from the *Acushnet* log

reading provided the background for *Moby Dick.* Just as his descriptions of life on the man-of-war ring true, so do those on the whaler, but for some of his most dramatic episodes he had to rely on the accounts of others. The final scene of *Moby Dick,* where the great white whale sends Ahab and the *Pequod* to the bottom, came largely from the little book by Owen Chase of Nantucket on the sinking of the whale ship *Essex.*

The *Essex* sailed from Nantucket on August 12, 1819, under the command of Captain George Pollard, Jr. After an uneventful voyage into the Pacific, on November 20, 1819, she found a pod of whales. While all boats were in pursuit, that of the mate, Owen Chase, was damaged by a whale and returned to the ship for repairs. As Chase prepared to lower again, a large sperm whale of about eighty-five feet, spouting on the surface, headed toward the ship. He attempted to avoid the beast which charged the ship at full speed, striking a tremendous blow. "The ship brought up violently as if she had struck a rock and trembled for a few minutes like a leaf." The whale then went under the vessel, scraping its back on the keel, and came up to leeward where it lay on the surface, apparently stunned. As the vessel began to settle and Chase was rigging the pumps, the whale swam slowly off for about one hundred yards and thrashed around, opening and closing his jaws in a rage. Chase was desperately attempting to deal with the emergency, when one of the sailors cried out, "Here he is—he is making for us again." Seeing the whale bearing down on them at a tremendous speed, Chase put the helm hard up, but the ship in her waterlogged condition did not answer the helm quickly. The whale smashed into the ship just under the cathead and completely stove in the bows. The men had time to rescue two quadrants, navigation books, a couple of compasses, and a small amount of bread and water. They barely got their whale boat over the side and clear when the ship "fell over to windward and settled down in the water." The shocked Captain Pollard approached in his boat, crying, "My God, Mr. Chase what is the matter?" Chase answered, "We have been stove by a whale." The ship did not sink immediately, and for three days they stood by the hulk, strengthening their whale boats and rigging them with masts and sails. Commanded by Captain Pollard and the two mates, the three boats with the total complement of twenty whalemen left the appalling scene. At the time of the disaster they were about twelve hundred miles from land. Two of the three boats survived, sailing over three thousand miles, with starving crews resorting to cannibalism before they were rescued.[4]

NEW ENGLAND AND THE SOUTH SEAS

✳

If Melville's four years of South Sea wandering gave him the material for the bulk of his lasting literary output, it took only four months in the Hawaiian Islands to mark the turning point in the career of the man whom many regard as America's greatest literary figure. Before his visit to Hawaii he was a newspaper man; shortly afterward he was a writer of rapidly increasing stature. Mark Twain cannot by any stretch of the imagination be considered a New Englander, but he lived the last years of his life in Redding, Connecticut, and died there in his home, Stormfield. When he was building this house, only two years before his death, the people of Hawaii sent him an elaborately carved mantelpiece of hard, curly, koa wood, together with a carving of breadfruit and leaves to go above it; it was installed on Twain's seventy-third birthday.

Mark Twain's twenty-five letters to the Sacramento *Union* on the Hawaiian Islands and their personalities were an important part of his rising stature as a writer and humorist, and his lectures on them for many years afterwards were among his most popular. His prose poem on the Islands has been reprinted hundreds of times and is a standard feature in Hawaiian tourist literature. It is one of the best expressions of the feeling Hawaii or any of the Polynesian islands generates in those who visit them.

No alien land in all the world has any deep, strong charm for me but that one, no other land could so longingly and so beseechingly haunt me sleeping and waking, through half a lifetime, as that one has done. Other things leave me, but it abides; other things change, but it remains the same. For me its balmy airs are always blowing, its summer seas flashing in the sun, the pulsing of its surf-beat is in my ear; I can see its garlanded crags, its leaping cascades, its plumy palms drowsing by the shore, its remote summits floating like islands above the cloud rack; I can feel the spirit of its woodland solitudes, I can hear the plash of its brooks; in my nostrils still lives the breath of flowers that perished twenty years ago.[5]

How delightfully Mark Twain's reaction to the Hawaiian Islands compares with that of Boston's chronic pessimist, Henry Adams, who with the artist John La Farge stopped there for about a month in 1890! Adams appreciated the beauties of the place: the long line of white surf, the sweeping blue ocean, the color, the space, the light, the rainbows. But, after writing in one of his letters about a moonlight night, he adds, "we went to bed, with doubts of centipedes and quad-rapeds." And, after an interesting drive, "but the stories of cockroaches, and centipedes, not to mention scorpions, make one's teeth chatter; and the mosquitoes, at night, are as bad as at Beverly."[6] In making a trip over to the big island to see the volcano he was seasick on the steamer, and, after he reached Punaluu Landing, wrote, "As I detest mountains, abominate volcanoes, and execrate the sea, the effort is a tremendous one; but I make it from a sense of duty to the savages who killed Captain Cook just about here a century ago. One good turn deserves another. Perhaps they will kill me. I never saw a place where killing was less like murder." On the steamer he was offered mangoes, pineapples, and other tropical fruit, "all which I am somewhat too nauseated to eat. Our steamer is filled with plaintive-looking native women— the old-gold variety—who vary in expression between the ferocious look of the warriors who worshipped Captain Cook and then killed him, and the melancholy of the generation obliged to be educated by missionaries." He was disappointed in the Volcano House and in the great crater, but, returning on the steamer, relented a little and said, "I take it all back. Hawaii is fascinating, and I could dream away months here." This exuberance did not last long. While crossing the island, he wrote, "When I dismounted and entered the dirty little restaurant, I found our two young ladies eating supper at a dusky table. They had ordered for me a perfectly raw fresh fish, and the old-goldest of the two showed me how to eat it, looking delightfully savage as she held the dripping fish in her hands and tore its flesh with her teeth." Later that evening, however, he enjoyed the moonlight while the Hawaiians strummed guitars and sang Hawaiian songs, only one of which he liked very much. In general, he tells his correspondent, if she wants to get a better impression of the Islands she should read Isabelle Bird Bishop's travels in the Sandwich Islands of which he says, "I have carefully avoided looking at her remarks, for I know that she always dilates with correct emotion, and I yearn only for the incorrect ones; but you will surely see Islands of soundest principles—travellers' principles, I mean—if you read Miss Bird, who will tell you all that I ought to have seen and felt, and for whom the volcano behaved so well."[7] Further, on the volcano, he said, "To irritate me still more, we are now assured that the lake of fire by which we sat unmoved, became very active within four-and-twenty hours afterwards. These are our lucks. I never see the world as the world ought to be." He and La Farge had an audience with King Kalakaua on September 26, after which Adams commented that the king "talks quite admirable English in a charming voice; has admirable manners; and—forgive me just this once more— seems to me a somewhat superior Chester A. Arthur; a type surprisingly common among the natives. To be sure His Majesty is not wise, and he has—or is said to have—vices, such as whisky and—others; but he is the only interesting figure in the government. . . . I would not be thought to prefer Kalakaua to Benjamin Harrison, but I own to finding him a more amusing subject."8

Adams and La Farge went on to Samoa, where they arrived in early October, and were the guests of the American Consul, Harold Marsh Sewall. Adams enjoyed his stay in Samoa. He liked the people, and, the first time the dancing girls came out, he said, "La Farge's spectacles quivered with emotion and gasped for sheer inability to note everything at once." They visited King Malietoa, who impressed Adams as "not *opéra bouffe,* or Kalakaua."9 They were also impressed with Malietoa's rival, Mataafa, who gave them a long speech in the best Samoan manner.

On October 16 Sewall took Adams and La Farge to call on Robert Louis Stevenson. They found him living in a shanty about an hour's horseback ride up in the hills. "As we reached the steps a figure came out that I cannot do justice to. Imagine a man so thin and emaciated that he looked like a bundle of sticks in a bag, with a head and eyes morbidly intelligent and restless. He was costumed in a dirty striped cotton pyjamas. The baggy legs tucked into coarse knit woolen stockings, one of which was bright brown in color, the other a purplish dark tone." Adams liked Stevenson but was appalled by his hardy life. It was a life for a healthy man, "but a Scotchman with consumption can defy fatigue and danger." Stevenson said that he would never leave the island and could not understand how any man able to live in the South Seas would ever consent to live elsewhere.10 They had a long discussion on Polynesian morals on which Adams remarks, "I can easily understand getting very mixed up about Polynesian morals, for I feel that the subject is a deep one, and the best informed whites seem perplexed about it; but I remember how much poor Okakura was perplexed by the same subject in America." He further says, "Every married woman here, after a few years residence with her husband, returns to her father with half the children, and lives as she likes. I think the custom will commend itself at once to New York society, not to mention that of Washington." He then dryly remarks, "Let it be enough that we have become Samoans in spirit and only abstain from adopting their dress and habits out of pure moral conviction that the Congregational Church is the only safe guide in those matters."[11]

46. U.S. Consulate in German Samoa in 1900

SEARCHING FOR PARADISE

Adams liked the songs of the people, their feasts, their entertainments, and their naturalness, but he did not particularly relish the food. When treated to kava for the first time, he describes it as, "a queer lingering, varying, aromatic, arumatic, Polynesian, old-gold flavor, that clings to the palate like creosote or coal-oil. I drank the milk of the green cocoa-nut to wash it off, but all the green cocoa-nuts in the ocean could not wash out that little taste." I suspect that much of Adams' enjoyment of Samoa was due to the fact that Stevenson was there and that Sewall entertained him with a series of dinners, parties, and expeditions. At one dinner he met Dorence Atwater, American Consul at Tahiti, a Yankee who had married a native. Adams observed, "for taking the fun out of everything, a Yankee matches a Scotchman, and Mr. Atwater has perhaps been long enough in the South Seas to reach the universal lava-foundation of commonplace." (It was Atwater, however, who arranged for Adams and La Farge to stay with his brother-in-law, Tati Salmon, a member of one of the most prominent Tahitian families.) The constant chatter about the minutiae of local politics did not impress Adams. "After several times expressing myself in my usual offensive and dogmatic manner on the character of this small beer, I have sunk into silence more or less sullen, and let the talk go on as it will." Before leaving Samoa, he arranged for a dinner party to which every eligible person on the island was invited. "Regardless of expense, to throw all previous Samoan entertainments into outer darkness."[12]

Adams arrived in Tahiti when the island was at a low point in population and in the condition of the natives. He found them sad compared with the gay Samoans. "Papeete is one of those ideal spots which have no fault except that of being insupportable," and, "lovely as it is, it gets on my nerves at last."

However, he and La Farge made a trip to Tautira where they camped out a while, and after a few months he was able to write "Tahiti is lovely; the climate is perfect; we have made a sort of home here; and I never shall meet another spot so suitable to die in." Adams was bored by the lack of intellectual stimulation ("Generally eternal sunshine falls on eternal cocoanuts")[13] until he persuaded one of the old ladies in the house of Salmon to dictate the ancient stories, history, traditions, and genealogy of her people. This he enjoyed, and his manuscript was later privately printed.[14] The two travelers left Tahiti in early June on a steamer which stopped briefly at Rarotonga, and then went on to Fiji where they lived with Sir John Thurston, governor-general of the island, until July 23. Henry Adams' reaction to the South Seas was certainly not the same as Melville's, but his letters contain some of the most penetrating observations on the islands.

No place on earth seemed more like paradise to the eighteenth-century explorers than the islands of Polynesia. New England whalers, traders, and naval men had the same reaction—a reaction that colored the reports and books written in the early nineteenth century. Day after day, week after week of beautiful, tropical trade-wind weather can be boring on a modern ship. Imagine how much more boring it could be when those weeks lengthened into months on a sailing vessel!

My own opinion, as a New Englander in the South Seas, is that the appeal of the islands, the impact of beauty unrivaled and climate of unsurpassed gentleness, perpetuates the myth of paradise. But I must admit that I found much in common with Henry Adams. Except for an occasional dish and the fresh fruit, the food is appalling; one can throw a saddle on the cockroaches; the scorpions, centipedes, and spiders are either dangerous or revolting. The beaches are not soft on the feet; one treads warily in the water for fear of the poisonous barb of the little fish that huddle in the sand. And one picks up cone

47. Tahitians carving wooden bowls

shells with equal caution if at all, for fear of the deadly cloth of gold. There are devils in paradise! There is also a lack of cultural entertainment—with no libraries, no theaters, no symphonies, no newspapers worthy of the name. One lives in an inconvenient capsule of ribald sophistication—in a haze of native beer, rum, taro, fish, roast suckling pig, and amiable people. For most Yankees, accustomed to stimulating climate, activities, and interests, it becomes after a while a living death of a dreary, lotus-eating sort; only a few adjust and remain.

NEW ENGLAND AND THE SOUTH SEAS

One gets a descriptive similarity and continuity throughout the range of South Sea books. Because some of the writers have been skillful and distinguished literary men, the paradise tradition has become imbedded in literature. This has influenced others to travel in the Pacific and write their books.

The allure of the islands still produces its annual crop of books, and if the writers are neither Melvilles nor Adamses, they are in the tradition. Neither Nordhoff nor Hall was a New Englander, but both were partly of that ancestry and their books were published in Boston. At least two Yankee writers are making their homes in Tahiti today: William A. Robinson, sailor, adventurer, writer, and scholar; and William S. Stone, whose *Ship of Flame* is as fine a piece of writing on a native legend as has ever been done. And there are others toiling in the literary vineyards scattered the length and breadth of the Pacific, charmed by its beauties, its climate, and its people, building up the South Sea legend, and searching for paradise.

SEARCHING FOR PARADISE

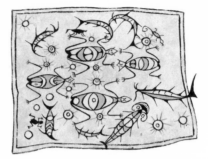

VIII ~

SHADOWS AND CONCLUSIONS

More than a century and a half has passed since the first New Englanders entered the South Seas. During this time the relationship between the two groups has been cruel, exploiting, tumultuous, solicitous, and seductive—but never dull. In spite of significant changes for good and for evil in these widely separated places, each has retained its distinctive identity.

The effects of the South Sea Islander and Yankee upon one another, while by no means of equal importance, were not entirely one-sided. Probably the greatest personal impact of islanders on New England was made by the Hawaiians and others who came to study at the Mission School in Cornwall, Connecticut; these young men caught the popular fancy at a time when there was intense interest in "converting the heathen" of foreign lands. Other natives shipped on American vessels but, lost among polyglot crews, their influence was negligible. The Polynesians were excellent sailors. Marquesans, New Zealanders, Tahitians, and especially Hawaiians were employed by the hundreds on traders and whalers, although most of them remained in the Pacific area when the ships returned to New England. Even most of the young Hawaiians who studied in the missionary school were originally seamen, and some of them fought for the United States in the War of 1812. Thomas Hopu served on several privateers during that war, as did his fellow mission-ary student, William Kanui. Perhaps the most extensive naval service was that of George P. Kaumualii, son of the chief of Kauai; he was wounded in the engagement between the *Enterprise* and the *Boxer* and later served under Commodore Stephen Decatur on the *Guerriere* in the Mediter-ranean. The names of these men have survived because of their mission connection, but it is reasonably certain that dozens of other young Polyne-sians fought at sea during that war.

Unlike the Yankee impact in the South Seas, where the strong personal element has left its mark through lighter skins, New England names, and

48. Tahitian woman

SHADOWS AND CONCLUSIONS

traditions from Salem or other coastal towns, there was no comparable reverse effect. Nearly all the natives who visited New England returned home; those who did not usually succumbed to the rigorous climate or to diseases for which they had no immunity. A few half-breed children returned with their fathers. (Captain David Saunders brought his half-Fijian daughter to Salem as a little girl, and she lived there the rest of her life, a popular and respected member of the community.) But these exceptions had no noticeable effect on New England culture. Many more Americans left their descendants behind. Today in the Fijis, and elsewhere in the Pacific, it is not uncommon to find native families with Salem surnames.

The natural resources of the Pacific and its islands played no small part in the economic vitality of the New England seaboard. For decades sperm oil and other whale products made Nantucket, New Bedford, and New London prosperous, supplying money for gracious living in handsome houses and, eventually, the capital for textile mills and other industries. Similarly, sea otters, seals, sandalwood, bêche-de-mer, pearl shell, and tortoise shell contributed substantially, through the China trade, to the prosperity of Portsmouth, Newburyport, Salem, Boston, Cape Cod, and Providence.

Because of the long and distinguished connection between New England and the South Seas the historical and scientific resources relating to the Pacific in New England libraries and museums are of incomparable richness. The manuscript collections alone are enormous. There are large collections of logbooks of Pacific whalers and traders in the Providence Public Library, the Connecticut and Rhode Island Historical societies, Old Mystic Seaport, the New Bedford Public Library and the Whaling Museum in the same city, the Massachusetts Historical Society, the Kendall Whaling Museum in Sharon, the Peabody Museum, and the Essex Institute in Salem. Another aspect of the cultural interaction can be obtained from the vast archives of the American Board of Commissioners for Foreign Missions, one of the most fruitful mines for those doing research on the Hawaiian Islands and Micronesia and now deposited in Houghton Library at Harvard University. The Andover-Newton Theological School in Newton, Massachusetts, contains other missionary journals and papers. Nearly all of our great libraries have collections of business papers, letter-books, and account books of companies trading or whaling in the Pacific. Many clergymen, captains, traders, and even sailors kept private journals which are treasure-troves of information. Some journals and logs are illustrated with sketches or water colors of islands, harbors, and native scenes which illuminate the author's observations and have great intrinsic worth in themselves. The large and detailed journal kept by Charles Pickering of Salem, one of the scientists on Charles Wilkes United States Exploring Expedition, is now in the Massachusetts Historical Society. Several sealers, such as Edmund Fanning and Benjamin Morrell of Stonington, Connecticut, and Amasa Delano of Duxbury, published journals and reminiscences. Others still unpublished, such as John Eagleston's journal of his Fiji, Philippine, and China trading, are equally good.

There is material in the United States for scores of volumes that will further illuminate Pacific history. Nor should the student seeking primary source material on the South Seas stop at the great repositories. Nearly every local historical society within thirty miles of the Atlantic seaboard can produce something of interest. Each will have a few logs, a few papers, pictures, or portraits, and each will have some artifacts from the islands.

SHADOWS AND CONCLUSIONS

Some of the rarest native artifacts are found in obscure places. The men who went to the Pacific were inveterate collectors. Sailors have always brought back curiosities with which to impress their wondering, land-bound friends and relatives. When their ships touched at civilized countries such as China, India, and the European ports they usually bought, even in the late eighteenth and early nineteenth centuries, things that could be classified as tourist souvenirs. Even had they possessed the discrimination to do so, it would have been difficult for seamen to get material of a kind that would today be considered important from a scientific or artistic point of view. But anything they collected when they traded with Indians on the Northwest Coast or visited the Fijis for bêche-de-mer, the Hawaiian Islands for sandalwood, New Zealand

to replenish their ships' stores, Tahiti for rest and relaxation, or other islands where native culture had been little influenced by European contact is important to the modern ethnologist.

Here again the small institutions and historical societies produce surprising things. The Roger Williams Park Museum in Providence has a fine exhibition of early Polynesian pieces including two small, rare, carved Hawaiian figures. The

49. New Zealand *hei tiki*

Springfield Museum has one of the finest carved Easter Island birdmen in existence. In the Newburyport Historical Society I found a Fiji club with Maori carving, of which there are perhaps half a dozen known; and in the museum in Dover, New Hampshire, among a collection of American Indian fishhooks was a good example of a Marquesan bonito hook. Material can turn up anywhere. I saw half a dozen good Cook Island stone adze blades in a collection of Rhode Island Indian archaeological material, and a small well-carved Marquesan bone tiki was fished from the bottom of a well in Wiscasset, Maine.

New England attics still produce clubs, wooden pillows, fans, tapa cloth, spears, wooden bowls, carved coconuts, tapa beaters, and other treasures, although not in such abundance as formerly. These have enriched the collections of museums

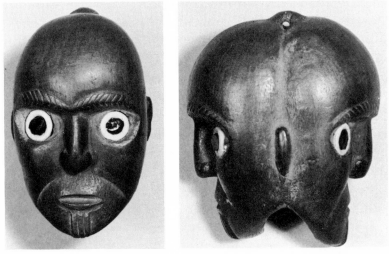

50. Easter Island carved Janus head

throughout the world. The great Hawaiian war god in Honolulu's Bishop Museum was once in Boston; several of its feather capes and cloaks were formerly the prized possessions of New England families. Much South Sea material collected by New Englanders has been given to the Smithsonian Institution,

SHADOWS AND CONCLUSIONS

where one also finds the collections made on the Wilkes Expedition. The Denver Museum of Art has, in recent years, built up a representative collection, some of which was acquired along the New England seaboard. Fine pieces are also located in the University Museum, Philadelphia, and the Brooklyn Museum. In the Whaling Museum at New Bedford there is a fine representative collection of Polynesian, Micronesian, and Fijian material which includes one of the largest and finest wooden bowls from Mangareva known.

Missionaries, as well as sailors and traders, contributed handsomely to this fund of documentary material. The superb collection made by the Reverend Asa Thurston and his wife, which contains several unique pieces, is now in the Peabody Museum of Salem. Other missionary collections formerly in the museum at the Andover-Newton Theological School are at Salem or—in the case of the brilliant feather capes, helmets, and kahilis—at the Peabody Museum at Harvard. The same institution also has from the same source two famous tapa figures showing tattooing designs of Easter Island. (So far as I know there is only one other of these figures in existence, at the Municipal Museum in Belfast, Northern Ireland.) Besides the missionary material, The Peabody Museum at Harvard contains a unique carved and painted figure of a fisherman's god from the Cook Islands. This collection, large and studded with important pieces, has other handsome carvings, including a rare wooden gong and headdresses from the Cook and Austral islands.

The largest and best-documented early collections from the Pacific in New England are found at the Peabody Museum in Salem. There is a good reason for this, this museum is the lineal descendant of the Museum of the East India Marine Society, a unique organization. The Salem East India Marine

Society was founded in 1799, and one of its avowed purposes was "to collect natural and artificial curiosities such as are to be found beyond Cape Horn and the Cape of Good Hope." In order to belong, a member had to be a Salem captain who had rounded one of the two great capes in command of a Salem ship. This was an extraordinary restriction and yet the Society, from the time it was founded until its Museum was taken over by the Peabody Trustees in the 1860's, had over four hundred members—an indication of the extent of foreign commerce in this small city on the North Shore of Massachusetts Bay. Each member was instructed to keep a journal to deposit with the Society and to bring back material for its museum. In 1821 the East India Marine Society went beyond this, and published a catalogue of its collections; another edition appeared in 1831. Thus the Pacific material collected at an early date was also unusually well documented.

Because of the domination of Salem men in the Fiji trade, the Peabody Museum collection from that group of islands is large and important. There is some pottery, many ornaments, bowls, canoe models, spears, tapa beaters, stacks of tapa, and almost literally cords of clubs. The rarest Fiji specimen is a model of a native temple made of sennit and having two towers. This is the only one of its kind in existence, all other temple models being modestly equipped with only one tower. The Salem collection is one of the world's three great Fijian collections; the others are at Cambridge University in England, and in the Fiji Museum at Suva.

The largest collection of early Micronesian material in the country is also at the Peabody Museum. It includes the only known lot of material of any size from the little island of Tobi, or Lord North Island, where Horace Holden, the tattooed man, was wrecked on the whaleship *Mentor*. The collection was

SHADOWS AND CONCLUSIONS

51. Gilbert Islander in coconut fiber armor

made by two Salem sailors whose ship stopped at that island for water.

But the museum's Polynesian collections are its most extensive and best documented and contain the greatest number of rarities. The East India Marine Society was directly responsible for organizing the tendency of men in strange ports to collect curiosities, and, because catalogues of those collections were published, the date of accession is known. The name of the donor is usually that of the collector, and the very logbooks of the voyages on which the specimens were acquired are frequently in the institution's library. Fifty-three men contributed specimens from the South Seas. The largest collections were given before 1830 by Nathaniel Page, William Putnam Richardson, William Richardson, Benjamin Vanderford, Thomas Meek, and Israel Williams, who made several voyages to the Pacific. There are substantial lots of material from Benjamin Wallis and John Eagleston. Captain Clifford Crowninshield of Salem and Captain Matthew Folger of Nantucket met somewhere in the

Pacific and pooled their keepsakes to give a collection jointly. John Fitzpatrick Jeffrey, an English captain who never saw Salem, heard of the newly established museum and gave his contribution to a Salem captain to be donated to the East India Marine Society in his name.

Some of the finest objects are single donations. A good example of this is the large Hawaiian carved figure donated by John T. Prince in 1846. Most of these figures were destroyed in the great desecration of the morais the year before the missionaries arrived in the Hawaiian Islands; three survive—in the Peabody Museum, the Bishop Museum, and the British Museum. Another single object of considerable importance but far less spectacular is a fan from Mangaia, Cook Islands, given before 1867. This is one of four known specimens; the only other one in the United States is at Wesleyan University in Middletown, Connecticut.

Two large wickerwork neck ornaments worn by Tahitian chiefs are of considerable rarity: one was given by William Eldredge in 1809, and

52. Seven-foot Hawaiian War God

SHADOWS AND CONCLUSIONS

the other by an unknown donor before 1821. These were scarce even in the flourishing days of Tahitian culture. There are several exquisitely carved fly whisk handles and an uncommon Tahitian bow and arrows. It was the good fortune of the Society's museum to receive a series of Marquesan fishhooks of a compound type, the only known specimens of the kind in existence. The single surviving example of a Marquesan malo or loin cloth was received from Israel Williams in 1802. Also from the Marquesas are two of the six known toggle harpoon points—one of human and the other of whale bone. Less rare but of considerable importance are the series of Hawaiian and Marquesan fans given by various individuals, as well as large series of the elaborate adzes from the Cook Islands and the carved paddles from the Austral Islands, nearly all with the known date of accession.

Such things as the only known Hawaiian tattooing needle and mallet, the only known piece of decorated Austral Island tapa, the only two Hawaiian shark tooth implements of a particular kind, the only old correct model of a Marquesan canoe, the only known Mangareva canoe with an outrigger, one of two known Mangareva clubs, the finest New Zealand Maori shark tooth scarifying knife in existence, are among the treasures of the Peabody Museum of Salem. There are any number of types of clubs, paddles, fans, ornaments, and household utensils that are among the half-dozen of each in existence. Weapons, of course, are especially well represented. Together with fishhooks they were the favorite objects for the captains to pick up, or possibly they were more readily obtainable than other things.

The origins of more recent additions to the collections in Salem stem from New Englanders' activities in the islands. The late Stephen W. Phillips of Salem, who was born in the

Hawaiian Islands, where his father was attorney general under the monarchy, added many important pieces, including the Goodale Hawaiian collection sent back to Marlborough, Massachusetts, in the early nineteenth century by the Reverend Asa and Lucy Thurston. The Samoan collection of the late Harold M. Sewall of Bath, Maine, was given by his widow and one of his sons. The John S. Emerson collection of Hawaiian antiquities was acquired for the Museum by the late Dr. Charles G. Weld of Boston. William A. Robinson, who made a voyage in a small boat around the world in the late 1920's, presented an admirable collection, including pottery and carvings from the Sepik River in New Guinea which he ascended for over two hundred miles.

The rich collections of manuscripts and artifacts at Salem and Harvard, supplemented by those in New Bedford, Providence, and New Haven, plus the many small but important deposits of material in various seaboard historical societies, comprise one of the world's greatest accumulations of documented material from the Pacific. They are an indispensable repository for the ethnologist, historian, and admirer of primitive art. Scholars will draw on these resources for years to come. As journals, correspondence, and reports are published, Pacific history will be further illuminated and we shall learn more about the culture of the South Sea Islanders.

Contact between New England and the South Seas has, in general, been an influence going from the more sophisticated culture to the simpler. This influence was not uniform throughout the area but varied, depending upon the kind and intensity of contact and with its persistence contingent upon its duration.

SHADOWS AND CONCLUSIONS

Then, too, the New England influences were in some instances poles apart (whalers and missionaries leave rather contrasting impressions), so different that they were bewildering to the Polynesian.

Yankee contact achieved its widest geographical extent in the first thirty years of the nineteenth century when American ships by the hundreds visited all of the major island groups. During this period they ranged the entire width of the Pacific from America to Indonesia and from Bering Strait to the Antarctic ice. The business that took them there was either whaling or one of the Pacific trades (sealing, sandalwood, or bêche-de-mer), usually subsidiary to the China trade complex.

That there was a lack of uniformity of contact from island group to island group appears evident from the following examples. Both traders and whalers frequented the Bay of Islands, New Zealand. There they contributed substantially to the native economy as well as to delinquency. More whalers than traders visited the Marquesas, and there was but one brief American missionary effort from Hawaii to these islands. Marquesans were apparently wilder, more unpredictable, and more truculent than most of the natives; therefore, obtaining fresh provisions and water was more dangerous than at Tahiti and other islands of the Society group. For this purpose and for general relaxation, Papeete was the favorite place of trader, whaler, and beachcomber alike as it has continued to be for the traveler ever since. In the Fijis it was a different matter. No one went there for his health; therefore, it was unpopular with whalers. But traders went there for profit for about forty years —first to Sandalwood Island (Vanua Levu) for that aromatic wood, and later to the other islands of the group where bêche-de-mer abounded. Here in these wild cannibal islands the influence of Yankee traders was perhaps equaled only by

English Wesleyan missionaries after they became established.

It was Hawaii, however, where New England influence was most intense, most active, most devastating, and most enduring. Beginning as a rest stop on the road to China, Hawaii quickly became a part of that trade as a producer of sandalwood, a home for Boston traders, a haven for New Bedford whalers, a show place for Calvinistic New England missionary efforts, a monarchy advised by Yankees.

The Hawaiian language was put into its written form by New England clergymen, who, while importing Christianity to the islands, also introduced the educational system in the public schools. Business enterprises founded by Yankees still flourish and the influence of men from their corner of the globe has been great in governmental circles. Yankee surnames abound, and the New England twang, only slightly modified, is the accent of the islands.

In the first third of the nineteenth century, American influence was strong to medium throughout the eastern and central Pacific. For various reasons—such as politics, economic fluctuations, or the decimation of natural resources—this influence changed over the years, dying out in some island groups and increasing, often with changing emphasis, in others. Absolutely none remains in the Marquesas, Tonga, or New Zealand. It has persisted to some extent on a tourist basis in the Society Islands. In eastern Samoa and all of Micronesia, except the Gilbert Islands, the United States bears political responsibility, and the early New England contacts provide no small amount of the background for our understanding of and good relations with the natives. The Hawaiian Islands have gone full way and have become our fiftieth state. The history of New England's half-century of commerce is one which combines to an extraordinary degree New England enterprise and hardi-

SHADOWS AND CONCLUSIONS

ness, hair-raising adventures, great monetary profits, and bold navigation in uncharted waters.

My personal experience illustrates one Yankee reaction to the South Seas. A New Englander, I viewed my first Polynesian island with elation and joy after a month-long voyage. Day after day, week after week of beautiful tropical trade-wind weather had passed. If it was boring on the freighter, imagine what it must have been on a sailing ship as weeks lengthened into months! It was a little after 3 P.M. when we raised the coral atoll of Napuka in the Tuamotus. From the time it came into view until it sank below the horizon I could not take my eyes off it. It looked just as it should have—like one of those silhouettes of islands found in logbooks, or more carefully done in the publications of explorers. We were too far away to see details, but on some of the little islets single palm trees stood out. Fascinated, I watched the atoll change in appearance as we steamed past. The tremendous surf breaking on the windward reef sent spray flying fifty feet into the air. At one point one could see over a long stretch of reef into the lagoon; at another the atoll looked like a necklace of green beads of varying lengths, with white columns of spray making jeweled spots along the string.

But coral atolls quickly faded into memory when the heart of paradise itself, Tahiti, rose out of the sea. Clearer, bluer, and more distinct it grew. As the steep, rugged mountains rose higher and higher, the Island of Moorea separated itself, and deep valleys took form. There were no clouds on the peaks which was unusual; even the highest were clear, Orahena and the Diadem standing sharply against the sky. The pilot with his straw hat came aboard. The pass was smooth and the sea flat; no swells were running. At the foot of the mountains nestled Papeete, with moored yachts, red-roofed houses, the Grand Hotel, and waterfront street spread out peacefully along the lagoon. Combine the color ashore and the color afloat with blue skies, tropical showers, cool nights for good sleeping, a constant daytime temperature, warm water, along with the amiable people—and what could be more persuasive to the chilled bones of a Yankee! No wonder New Englanders deserted their ships by the thousands to become beachcombers, bums, advisers to kings, raisers of potatoes!

Probably fewer New Englanders seek paradise in the South Seas today (excluding the Hawaiian Islands) than in the nineteenth century. And, unless they succumb to lethargy and indolence, most who go return. But the desire to flee to a South Sea paradise received an impetus with the return of Pacific veterans after World War II; for, though the charm of the islands could not obscure the conflict, it sometimes made it more bearable, and many an ex-serviceman has revisited them. Current popular literature still embalms the paradise myth, and doubtless with the coming of jets to the South Seas more authors will write more books in the same vein. Just as man must have his heroes, so must he have his Utopias!

Scarcely a Yankee alive in his hard-bitten environment does not dream of going to the South Seas. And this, it seems to me, is by no means entirely due to a general feeling of escapism. Some may be, but the memory of not-so-distant ancestors who went there for God, for profit, or for country lingers on. Tales of palm-clad islands, coral sands, blue seas, and pleasant climes heard in childhood; the faded ink of a treasured logbook or diary handed down in a family; the portrait of a missionary ancestor; a bit of sandalwood still aromatic in antiquity; a

SHADOWS AND CONCLUSIONS

tridacna shell in a garden—all evoke the desire to go to "the islands."

BIBLIOGRAPHY

NOTES

INDEX

BIBLIOGRAPHY

Adams, Henry. *Memoirs of Marau Taaroa, Last Queen of Tahiti.* Privately printed, 1893.

Alexander, W. D. *A Brief History of the Hawaiian People.* New York, 1899.

Anderson, C. R. *Melville in the South Seas.* New York, 1939.

Anderson, Rufus. *The Hawaiian Islands. Their Progress and Condition under Missionary Labors.* Boston, 1865.

Arago, J. *Voyage Autour du Monde.* Paris, n.d.

Barbeau, Marius. "All Hands Aboard Scrimshawing," *The American Neptune,* 12:99–122 (1952).

Bartlett, John. "A Narrative of Events in the Life of John Bartlett of Boston, Massachusetts, in the Years 1790–1793, During Voyages to Canton and the Northwest Coast of North America," in *The Sea, the Ship and the Sailor.* Salem, 1925, pp. 287–343.

Beaglehole, John C. *The Exploration of the Pacific.* London, 1934.

Beale, Thomas. *The Natural History of the Sperm Whale.* London, 1839.

Bishop, Isabelle Bird. *Six Months among the Palm Groves, Coral Reefs, and Volcanoes of the Sandwich Islands.* London, 1875.

Bingham, Hiram. *A Residence of Twenty-one Years in the Sandwich Islands or the Civil, Religious, and Political History of Those Islands.* Hartford and New York, 1849.

Bougainville, Lewis de. *A Voyage Round the World Performed by Order of His Most Christian Majesty, In the Years 1766, 1767, 1768, and 1769.* London, 1772.

Bradley, Harold W. *The American Frontier in Hawaii: The Pioneers, 1789–1843.* Stanford, Calif., 1942.

Brain, Belle M. *The Transformation of Hawaii.* New York, 1898.

Buck, Peter H. (Te Rangi Hiroa). *An Introduction to Polynesian Anthropology.* Bishop Museum Bulletin 187. Honolulu, 1945.

Chase, Owen. *Narrative of the Most Extraordinary and Distressing Shipwreck of the Whale-ship* Essex, *of Nantucket; Which was Attacked and Finally Destroyed by a Large Spermaceti-Whale, in the Pacific Ocean; With an Account of the Unparalleled Suffering of the Captain and Crew During a Space of Ninety-three Days at Sea, in Open Boats. In the Years 1819 and 1820.* New York, 1821.

Coan, Titus. *Life in Hawaii: An Autobiographic Sketch of Mission Life and Labors (1835–1881)*. New York, 1882.

Coffin, Robert. *The Last of the Logan: The True Adventures of Robert Coffin Mariner in the years 1854 to 1859 wherein are set forth His Pursuit of the Whale, his Shipwreck on Rapid Reef, his Life among the Cannibals of Fiji, and his Search for Gold in Australia, as Told by Himself and Now First Published,* ed. Harold W. Thompson. Ithaca, N.Y., 1941.

Colcord, Joanna C. *Songs of American Sailormen*. New York, 1938.

Cook, Captain James, and Captain James King. *A Voyage to the Pacific Ocean. Undertaken, by the Command of His Majesty, for Making Discoveries in the Northern Hemisphere . . . In the Years 1776, 1777, 1778, 1779, and 1780.* 3 vols., London, 1784.

Cook, Philip H. "Some Missionary Ships in the Pacific," *The American Neptune,* 10:264–279 (1950).

Cormack, Maribelle. *The Lady was a Skipper: The Story of Eleanor Wilson.* New York, 1956.

Darwin, Charles. *Narrative of the Surveying Voyages of His Majesty's Ships Adventure and Beagle.* Vol. III, London, 1839.

Davis, William Morris. *The Coral Reef Problem.* American Geographical Society, Special Publication No. 9. New York, 1928.

Day, A. G. *See* Kuykendall.

Delano, Amasa. *Narrative of Voyages and Travels, in the Northern and Southern Hemispheres; Comprising Three Voyages Round the World; Together with a Voyage of Survey and Discovery, in the Pacific Ocean and Oriental Islands.* Boston, 1817.

Derrick, R. A. *A History of Fiji.* Suva, 1957.

Dibble, Sheldon. *A History of the Sandwich Islands.* Honolulu, 1909.

Dodge, E. S. *The Hervey Islands Adzes in the Peabody Museum of Salem.* Salem, 1937.

———— *The Marquesas Islands Collection in the Peabody Museum of Salem.* Salem, 1939.

———— *The New Zealand Maori Collection in the Peabody Museum of Salem.* Salem, 1941.

———— *Northwest by Sea.* New York, 1961.

Dorsett, Edward Lee. "Hawaiian Whaling Days," *The American Neptune,* 14:42–46 (1954).

Dunbabin, Thomas. "New Light on the Earliest American Voyages to Australia," *The American Neptune,* 10:52–64 (1950).

Dwight, E. W. *Memoir of Henry Obookiah.* New York, [1819].

Eagleston Captain John Henry. Typescript journal of his voyages in Peabody Museum of Salem.

East India Marine Society letters, reports, and other MSS in Peabody Museum of Salem.

Endicott, William. *Wrecked Among Cannibals in the Fijis,* ed. L. W. Jenkins. Salem, 1923.

Fanning, Captain Edmund. *Voyages and Discoveries in the South Seas, 1792–1832.* Salem, 1924.

Ford, W. C., ed. *Letters of Henry Adams (1858–1891).* Boston, 1930.

Frear, W. F. *Mark Twain and Hawaii.* Chicago, 1947.

Freeman, Otis W., ed. *Geography of the Pacific.* New York, 1951.

Gardiner, J. Stanley. *Coral Reefs and Atolls.* London, 1931.

Halford, Francis John. *Nine Doctors and God.* Honolulu, 1954.

Harris, Sheldon H. "Mutiny on *Junior,*" *The American Neptune,* 21:110–129 (1961).

Hawaiian House Documents, 53d Congress, Ex. Doc. No. 48. Washington, D.C., 1893.

Hawkesworth, John. *An Account of the Voyages Undertaken by the Order of His Present Majesty for Making Discoveries in the Southern Hemisphere.* London, 1773.

Hohman, Elmo Paul. *The American Whaleman.* New York, 1928.

Holden, Horace. *A Narrative of the Shipwreck, Captivity, and Suffering of Horace Holden and Benjamin Nute.* Boston, 1836.

Howard, Leon. *Herman Melville: A Biography.* Berkeley and Los Angeles, 1951.

Hunnewell, James. *Journal of the Voyage of the* "Missionary Packet," *Boston to Honolulu, 1826.* Charlestown, Mass., 1880.

Hussey, Cyrus M. *See* Lay.

Im Thurn, Sir Evarard, and Leonard C. Wharton, eds. *The Journal of William Lockerby: Sandalwood Trader in the Fijian Islands During the Years 1808–1809: With an Introduction and Other Papers Connected with the Earliest European Visitors to the Islands.* The Hakluyt Society, series II, vol. LII. London, 1925.

Jarves, James J. *History of the Hawaiian or Sandwich Islands.* Boston, 1843.

[Jenkins, L. W.] *The Hawaiian Portion of the Polynesian Collections.* Salem, 1920.

Jewitt, John R. *Narrative of the Adventures and Sufferings of John R. Jewitt; Only Survivor of the Crew of the Ship* Boston, *During a Captivity of Nearly Three Years among the Savages of Nootka Sound: With an Account of the Manners, Mode of Living, and Religious Opinions of the Natives.* New York, 1815.

Kenny, Robert W. "The Maiden Voyage of *Ann and Hope,*" *The American Neptune,* 18:105–136 (1958).

Kenny, Robert W. "Yankee Whalers at the Bay of Islands," *The American Neptune*, 12:22–44. (1952).

——— ed. *The New Zealand Journal, 1842–1844, of John B. Williams of Salem, Massachusetts.* Salem, 1956.

King, Captain James. *See* Cook.

Krusenstern, A. J. von. *Voyage Round the World in the Years 1803, 1804, 1805, 1806, by Order of His Imperial Majesty Alexander the First on Board the Ships* Nadeshda *and* Neva. London, 1813.

Kuykendall, Ralph S. *The Hawaiian Kingdom 1778–1854.* Honolulu, 1947.

——— and A. G. Day. *Hawaii: A History.* New York, 1950.

La Farge, John. *Reminiscences of the South Seas.* New York, 1912.

Lay, William, and Cyrus M. Hussey. *A Narrative of the Mutiny on board the* Globe *of Nantucket, in the Pacific Ocean, Jan. 1824.* New London, 1828.

Ledyard, John. *Journal of Captain Cook's Last Voyage to the Pacific Ocean, and in Quest of a North-West Passage, Between Asia & America; Performed in the Years 1776, 1777, 1778, and 1779.* Hartford, 1783.

McNab, Robert. *The Old Whaling Days: A History of Southern New Zealand From 1830 to 1840.* Wellington, N.Z., 1913.

Meredith, J. C. *The Tattooed Man.* New York, 1958.

Morison, Samuel E. "Boston Traders in the Hawaiian Islands, 1789–1823," *Proceedings of the Massachusetts Historical Society*, 54:9–47 (1920).

——— *The Maritime History of Massachusetts.* Boston, 1921.

Morrell, Capt. Benjamin, Jun. *A Narrative of Four Voyages to the South Seas, North and South Pacific Ocean, Chinese Sea, Ethiopic and Southern Atlantic Ocean, Indian and Antarctic Ocean. From the Year 1822 to 1831.* New York, 1832.

Morrison, J. F. *A Chinese Commercial Guide, Consisting of a Collection of Details and Regulations Respecting Foreign Trade with China.* 3rd ed., Canton, 1848.

Oliver, Douglas L. *The Pacific Islands.* Cambridge, Mass., 1962.

[Oliver, James]. *Wreck of the* Glide. New York, 1848.

Osborn, Fairfield, ed. *The Pacific World.* New York, 1944.

Porter, Captain David. *Journal of a Cruise Made to the Pacific Ocean by Captain David Porter, in the United States Frigate* Essex *in the Years 1812, 1813, and 1814.* 2 vols., 2nd ed., New York, 1822.

Putnam, G. G. *Salem Vessels and Their Voyages.* Series IV, Salem, 1930.

Reynolds, J. N. *Voyage of the United States Frigate* Potomac, *under the Command of Commodore John Downes, During the Circumnavigation of the Globe, in the Years 1831, 1832, 1833, and 1834.* New York, 1835.

Reynolds, Stephen. *The Voyage of the* New Hazard, ed. F. W. Howay. Salem, 1938.

[Rickman, John]. *Journal of Captain Cook's last Voyage to the Pacific Ocean, on Discovery; performed in the Years 1776, 1777, 1778, 1779.* London, 1781.

Robertson, George. *The Discovery of Tahiti: A Journal of the Second Voyage of H.M.S.* Dolphin *Round the World, Under the Command of Captain Wallis, R.N., in the Years 1766, 1767, and 1768,* ed. Hugh Carrington. The Hakluyt Society, series II, vol. XCVIII. London, 1948.

Samoan House Documents. 50th Congress, Ex. Doc. No. 238, 1888; 53d Congress, Ex. Doc. No. 97, 1895. Washington, D.C.

Scammon, Charles M. *The Marine Mammals of the North-western Coast of North America.* San Francisco, 1874.

Smith, Bernard. *European Vision and the South Pacific, 1768–1850.* Oxford, 1960.

Snow, Elliot, ed. *The Sea, the Ship and the Sailor.* Salem, 1925.

Sparks, Jared. *The Life of John Ledyard, the American Traveller; Comprising Selections From His Journals and Correspondence.* Cambridge, Mass., 1828.

Stackpole, Edouard A. *The Sea-Hunters.* New York, 1953.

Starbuck, Alexander. *History of the American Whale Fishery from its Earliest Inception to the Year 1876.* Waltham, Mass., 1878.

Stevenson, Robert Louis. *A Footnote to History.* London, 1892.

Stewart, C. S. *A Visit to the South Seas in the U.S. Ship* Vincennes, *During the Years 1829 and 1830; with Scenes in Brazil, Peru, Manilla, the Cape of Good Hope, and St. Helena.* 2 vols., New York, 1831.

Stone, William S. *The Ship of Flame.* New York, 1945.

Sullivan, Josephine. *A History of C. Brewer and Company Limited: One Hundred Years in the Hawaiian Islands, 1826–1926.* Boston, 1926.

Thompson, Harold W., ed. *The Last of the* Logan. Ithaca, N. Y., 1941.

Thurston, Lucy G. *Life and Times of Mrs. Lucy G. Thurston, Wife of Rev. Asa Thurston, Pioneer Missionary to the Sandwich Islands Gathered from Letters and Journals Extending Over a Period of More than Fifty Years.* Ann Arbor, 1882.

Townsend, Charles H. "The Distribution of Certain Whales as Shown by Logbook Records of American Whaleships," *Zoologica: Scientific Contributions of the New York Zoological Society,* vol. 19, no. 1. New York, 1935.

[Wallis, Mary]. *Life in Fiji.* Boston, 1851.

Warriner, Francis. *Cruise of the United States Frigate* Potomac *Round the World, During the Years 1831–1834.* New York, 1835.

Waterhouse, Joseph. *The King and People of Fiji.* London, 1866.

Weaver, Raymond M. *Herman Melville, Mariner and Mystic.* New York, 1921.

Wharton, Leonard C. *See* Im Thurn.

BIBLIOGRAPHY

Wheeler, Daniel. *Extracts From the Letters and Journal of Daniel Wheeler, While Engaged in a Religious Visit to the Inhabitants of Some of the Islands of the Pacific Ocean, Van Dieman's Land, New South Wales, and New Zealand.* Philadelphia, 1840.

Whitehill, Walter M. "George Crowninshield's Yacht *Cleopatra's Barge*," *The American Neptune,* 13:235–251 (1953).

Wilkes, Charles. *Narrative of the United States Exploring Expedition During the Years 1838, 1839, 1840, 1841, 1842.* 5 vols. and atlas, Philadelphia, 1845.

Williams, Thomas, and James Calvert. *Fiji and the Fijians.* 2 vols., London, 1858.

Wood, Gordon L. *The Pacific Basin.* Oxford, 1930.

Zimmerman, Heinrich. *Reise um die Welt, mit Capitain Cook.* Mannheim, 1781.

NOTES

CHAPTER I.
THE GREAT SOUTH SEA

1. Bougainville, p. 467.
2. Most of the facts on Ledyard's life are based on Sparks.
3. Ledyard, p. 70.

CHAPTER II.
HUNTING THE CACHALOT

1. Colcord, p. 191.
2. Morison, *Maritime History,* p. 322.
3. Darwin, pp. 496–497.
4. Snow, p. 181.
5. Thompson, p. 57.
6. Hohman, p. 33.
7. Kenny, "Yankee Whalers," p. 39.
8. *Ibid.,* pp. 32–33.
9. Dorsett, p. 44.
10. Wheeler, p. 62.
11. *Ibid.,* pp. 65–66.
12. *Ibid.,* pp. 105–106.
13. *Ibid.,* p. 119.
14. Wilkes, p. 498.
15. Harris, pp. 110–129.
16. Meredith, p. 81.
17. Wilkes, p. 484.

CHAPTER III.
SEA OTTERS, SEALS, AND SANDALWOOD

1. Jewitt, p. 67.
2. Morison, *Maritime History,* p. 57.
3. Jewitt, p. 15.
4. Fanning; Morrell; Delano.
5. Fanning, p. 86.
6. Morrell, p. 30.
7. Delano, pp. 377–378.
8. *Ibid.,* p. 394.
9. *Ibid.,* pp. 397–398.
10. *Ibid.,* pp. 467–468.
11. Morison, *Maritime History,* p. 262.
12. Bingham, p. 126.
13. Whitehill, pp. 11–12.

CHAPTER IV.
BÊCHE-DE-MER AND CANNIBALS

1. Im Thurn.
2. Derrick, p. 43.
3. Fanning, p. 327.
4. Wilkes, III, 221.
5. *Ibid.,* p. 219.
6. Wallis.
7. Waterhouse, p. 329.
8. Williams, p. 210.
9. *Ibid.,* p. 212.
10. Waterhouse, p. 70.
11. Williams, p. 75.
12. Waterhouse, p. 78.
13. Wilkes, III, 67.

CHAPTER V.
WITH COURAGE AND ZEAL

1. Dwight.
2. Jarves, pp. 218–221.
3. Alexander, p. 189.
4. Hunnewell, p. xxii.
5. *Ibid.,* p. 3.
6. Cook, P. H., p. 274.
7. *Ibid.,* p. 276.
8. *Ibid.,* p. 277.
9. *Ibid.,* p. 264.
10. *Ibid.,* p. 277.

CHAPTER VI.
YANKEES IN ISLAND POLITICS

1. Alexander, p. 195.
2. Halford, p. 94.
3. *Ibid.,* p. 110.
4. *Ibid.,* p. 118.
5. Sullivan, p. 30.
6. *Ibid.,* p. 93.

CHAPTER VII.
SEARCHING FOR PARADISE

1. Hawkesworth.
2. For example, Leyard; Rickman; Zimmerman.
3. Morison, *Maritime History,* pp. 41–42.
4. Chase.
5. Frear, p. 217.
6. Ford, pp. 407, 408.
7. *Ibid.,* pp. 408–409, 411, 413. See also Bishop.
8. Ford, pp. 414, 415.
9. *Ibid.,* pp. 418, 420.
10. *Ibid.,* pp. 425, 430.
11. *Ibid.,* pp. 426–427, 430–431.
12. *Ibid.,* pp. 418, 453, 456.
13. *Ibid.,* pp. 468, 469, 482, 487.
14. Adams.

INDEX

INDEX

INDEX

INDEX

INDEX

INDEX

INDEX

INDEX

INDEX

INDEX

Typography and design by Burton Jones
Drawings by Beryl Bailey Jones
Endleaf map by Samuel H. Bryant

This book was set on the Fotosetter in 12 point Baskerville type,
leaded 2 points, by Graphic Services, Inc., York, Pennsylvania
Printed by the Murray Printing Co., Forge Village, Massachusetts
Bound by Colonial Press, Inc., Clinton, Massachusetts

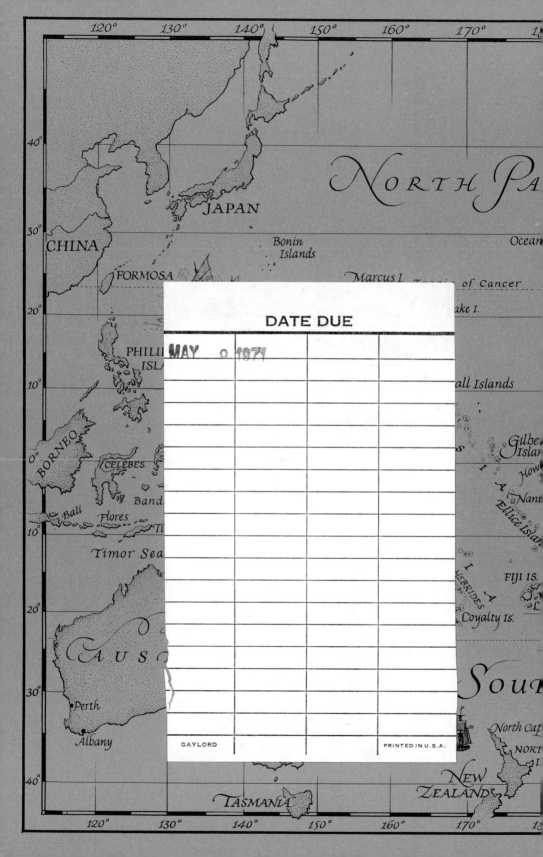

DATE DUE